OFFCUTS 2:
Sketches and Stories from The Shed

Armour

OFFCUTS 2:
Sketches and Stories from the Shed

ST JOHN'S OXLEY COMMUNITY MEN'S SHED

Bill Barker
Jim Pascoe
Trevor Armstrong
Darryl Dymock
James Vernon
Dave Shearer
George Pugh
John Brown
Bill Thirkill

Sketches:
Peter Darmody, Anthony Durrington,
Brian Goeldner, George Pugh,
Dave Shearer, Alan Smith

Offcuts 2: Sketches and Stories from the Shed

St John's Oxley Community Men's Shed

© Individual contributors 2022

Published by Armour Books
P. O. Box 492, Corinda QLD 4075

Interior Design and Typeset by Beckon Creative

Cover Images: Original artwork by Peter Darmody

Illustrations:
Train, Peter Darmody, page vi
Vietnam, Peter Darmody, page 18
Yacht, Alan Smith, page 35
Drongo, Anthony Durrington, page 45
Queenslander, Alan Smith, page 60
St John's Oxley, Peter Darmody, page 74
Matchbox, Dave Shearer, page 81
Lighthouse, Brian Goeldner, page 82
Police Car, George Pugh, page 90
Birds, Anthony Durrington, page 95
Untitled, Alan Smith, page 109
Untitled, Peter Darmody and Brian Goeldner, page 110
David, Anthony Durrington, page 127
Feet up, Anthony Durrington, page 135

ISBN: 978-1-925380-51-4

A catalogue record for this book is available from the National Library of Australia

All rights reserved. No part of this publication may be reproduced, stored in, or introduced into a retrieval system, or transmitted, in any form, or by any means (electronic, mechanical, photocopying, recording or otherwise) without the prior written permission of the publisher.

Note: Australian spelling and grammar conventions are used throughout this book.

Introduction

WELCOME TO THE SECOND ANTHOLOGY of stories from the Writers Group at St John's Oxley Community Men's Shed, *Offcuts 2: Sketches and Stories from the Shed*.

We had a wonderful reception to our 2021 issue, and I've no doubt this one will be just as popular. *Offcuts 2* includes not only the usual array of intriguing, amusing, amazing and unlikely stories, but this year we've added photos from the writers and sketches from the Men's Shed Drawing Group.

I'm indebted to Peter Darmody for convening the Drawing Group and encouraging the members to exercise the drawing talent that is displayed in the book. We also have Peter to thank for the unique artwork on the cover. (No doubt Shed members will be trying to identify themselves in the scene.)

I want to acknowledge the encouragement of the Writers Group by the other Shed members, especially the President, Martin Rankine, and by Rev Morris Rangiwai, Sherwood Anglican Parish. We are also grateful to Armour Books for their continuing publishing support for the Writers Group's endeavours.

As convenor of that group, I've been impressed by the members' persistence and passion in writing and their constancy in turning up every fortnight. They willingly share their stories with their fellow writers and also sometimes with the whole Shed. During the year, professional editor Ian Mathieson generously gave us some tips for improving the quality of our writing.

When you read the brief biographies of the contributors to *Offcuts 2*, you will see what a diverse mob we are. That diversity is a reminder that we all have stories to tell. While some tales may seem more exciting or amazing than others, our stories make up our lives. They make us who we are today. The longer we live, the more stories we have to tell.

Many of the writers of these stories say they are writing for their families. That's no doubt true, and I hope that those families and the wider community will enjoy these yarns and appreciate the effort the writers have put in.

However, we are also writing for ourselves, telling ourselves our stories from the past, trying to make sense of those experiences (and sometimes struggling to recall them accurately!) We all need stories to keep us going, both as writers and readers. Here, the sketches are a bonus.

I'm confident the stories in *Offcuts 2* will keep readers going for quite a while, and that will sustain the writers as well.

Darryl Dymock

Convenor, Oxley Men's Shed Writers Group

Editor

Train – Peter Darmody

Contents

Introduction v

Bill Barker 1
   THE CALL UP 1
   KAPOOKA 5
   A DRIVE IN THE COUNTRYSIDE 9

Jim Pascoe 19
   A DAY AT THE PUB 19
   AN OCEAN VOYAGE 24
   WORKING IN THE 1974 BRISBANE FLOODS 30

Trevor Armstrong 36
   A HITCHHIKER'S GUIDE TO TRAVELLING TO OTHER INTERESTING PLACES 36
   HELPING MANAGE OUR LOCAL NATURAL ENVIRONMENT .. 38
   FLOOD EXPERIENCES 40
   PENNYWORT CREEK HISTORY AND REHABILITATION 42

Darryl Dymock 46
   WHITE CHALK AND JUNIPER GREEN 46
   A LIFETIME OF LEARNING AND A LOVE OF WORDS 53

James Vernon 61
   SCHOOL AND OTHER DISTRACTIONS 61

Dave Shearer 75
    LIGHTHOUSE SERVICE 75
    ALWAYS CHECK THE MENU! 78

George Pugh 83
    MAJOR CRIMES 83
    BAD LUCK BANK ROBBERIES 87
    ATTACK ON A YOUNG WOMAN 91

John Brown 96
    THE SMELL OF NEW-MOWN HAY 96
    HAY GROWING, AND HARVESTING 101
    LOADING THE BALES AND STACKING 106

Bill Thirkill 111
    CAMPING TOURS OF RUSSIA IN THE SIXTIES 111
    LUNCH WITH KING HUSSEIN 116
    THE LURE OF THE DEEP 120
    AFRICA AND ORANGES 122

Contributors 129

Sketches and Stories from the Shed

Bill Barker

THE CALL-UP

Compulsory National Service began for me in a slightly different way to the majority of those men chosen by the ballot system. I was notified of my call-up in the first half of 1966. I did not have to report for duty as my ecclesiastical studies exempted me for as long as I continued my studies to completion. After two and a half years, I realised this was not to be my life's work.

Knowing that I had the National Service call-up pending, I took a job at the West End pub to give me some income while I waited. During my time at the pub, I tried the Airforce as a delaying tactic but it did not work for long. As it turned out, that short time as the pub junior manager gave me my future non-infantry role as a member of the Royal Australian Army Services Corps.

On 17 July 1968, I was required to present myself to the Officer Commanding at Northern Command Personnel Depot, Ashgrove, at 0800 hours, to begin my two years of compulsory service. I spent five days there doing not too much except keeping out of people's way. The barracks was never set up to handle one lone recruit.

I made myself busy doing nothing, with the help of the duty sergeant. Over coffee one day he asked, 'Recruit Barker, do you play rugby union?'

'Most certainly, ever since my early primary school days. I have two brothers who toured with the Wallabies.'

'Then make sure you pack your footy boots and rugby shorts.'

This was the only conversation I can remember from that week. The outcomes from listening to him and taking his advice had very pleasant consequences.

On the fourth day I was informed I was to report the next day for departure for recruit training. I had been going home each night, travelling by tram each way with a short walk, carrying all the gear back and forth that I was taking to Kapooka basic training base, in southern New South Wales. I was departing on the evening train from South Brisbane Station the next evening. All this was my first experience of military organisation and movement.

The train was overnight to Sydney and then by bus through Wagga Wagga to the Kapooka base. Our pre-arranged compartment held one other recruit. He did not want to talk, and just curled up and pretended to sleep for most of the trip. All I came to know was that he was a non-combatant on religious grounds.

Unknown to us both, there was a mixture of other Queenslanders and New South Welshmen on the train, which we only discovered when we reached Sydney. At Central Station we were all ushered onto a bus for the trip to Kapooka. It seemed that I was not the only left-over who did not end up at Singleton, where Queensland National Servicemen were usually sent for recruit training. Graham Bate, who features later in my story, must have been on the bus as well.

KAPOOKA

After a rather dull trip and a couple of stops for a break and an Army-paid-for lunch, we arrived at Kapooka. I had no idea of the time except that it was dark and very cold. From the bus we were ushered into the largest dining room, the mess, that I had ever seen. It dwarfed my boarding school dining room and could have been used for an indoor football field.

Now the regimentation began. We were ordered into single file and moved towards the counter to collect a tray, plates, cutlery and a cup. The food was placed on the plates with not much delicacy and we moved to tables that had been designated for us. We were very hungry after a cold drive from Sydney and the food was much better than boarding school food and there was more of it. To my amazement there must have been a couple of hundred recruits in the mess hall, with only low conversation to be heard.

As we ate, an officer was walking around the tables with seemingly nothing in mind except to keep tabs on us. Then, above the quiet mumble that existed from the tables, came his authoritarian voice.

'Does any one here play rugby union?'

I raised my hand a little and said, 'I do.'

Out of the great number that were there, I was the only one to respond.

'Do you have footy shorts and boots?'

'Yes.'

'Yes, sir,' was the officer's response, my first experience of Army protocol. 'Good, you are to be down on the ovals at 1500 hours, 3 pm for the uneducated, tomorrow and every Tuesday and Thursday for training. Tell the training officer (they were only corporals, so I found out) that you have to be there, it is an order. I do not care what you are doing, just be there. Clear?'

'Yes, sir.' I was learning.

From that Saturday until the end of the footy season, I boarded an Army bus on Saturday morning for a day out of camp, travelling the area around Wagga Wagga playing rugby with the Army team, and having a beer or two as well. All the other recruits at Kapooka had a day's training and were not allowed alcohol until the last weeks of basic training.

With the meal completed, the officer in control began to direct what was to happen next. The corporals who would mentor the various training platoons began to assemble, and our names were read out in platoon order. As we ended up on the top floor of the last barracks, we were the last to leave the mess hall.

We collected our bags and followed the corporal in rough military order down the path to our building where we were allocated rooms, four to a room. With the non-combatant from the train trip and two others, I was allocated the first room on the left. The others followed in like manner. There were at least 40 of us (because 40 survived basic training) and the corporal had his room at the far end. Our beds were made military style for us, so we collapsed into bed after a long day and slept well in our civilian gear.

At 0600 hours basic training began with the command to assemble down on the small parade ground in front of our building in what clothes we had. It was freezing. Our names were read out, followed by the compulsory response, 'Here, sir.'

Our platoon commander was on parade and gave a welcoming pep-talk. He was a young first lieutenant.

My room is the second window, top floor from the right.

We were then taken back up to our rooms and with the assistance of a couple of other corporals, each room was shown how the beds were to be made and how clothes were to be folded in our cupboards. The demonstration bed was stripped and we all had to try to emulate the making. Having completed our first attempt at bed making, breakfast came next and we were told to be ready at 0800 hours to begin the day.

The day was an orientation day. It involved remembering our regimental number, collecting our uniforms and webbing. The slouch hat size was a problem for me but eventually they found one that fitted. There were two pairs of boots and the essential boot cleaning kit and Brasso to keep the shine on the brass for the dress uniform. There was another medical check as we went through the Q Store.

Having deposited the clothing and boots in our lockers, we were off to the armoury to be issued with a SL1A1 Self-Loading Rifle (SLR) and cleaning kit. We were told to memorise our rifle number. By the end of basic training I had already smashed my first rifle while completing an obstacle course and had to remember another rifle number. There was the compulsory photograph with the regimental number showing.

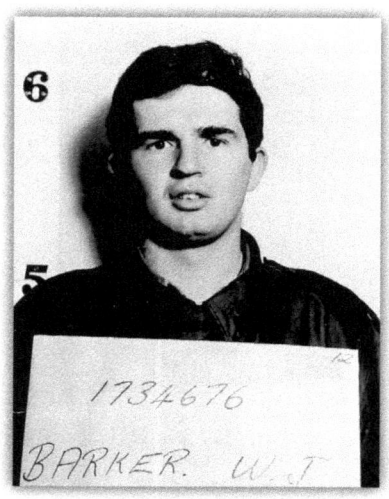

My first army photograph

By the end of the first day, we had collected all our gear, marched in an unmilitary way around most of the base, and been told quite often, in explicit terms, that we were not following orders in a regimental manner and that we had to shape up. The corporals' language was a little more colourful as the day progressed, and at times they appeared to be trying to outdo one another.

The day ended about mid-afternoon with the order to iron, fold and store our gear neatly with the rounded side showing and be ready for inspection by 0800 hours the next morning. No pressure. Ironing, washing and polishing became a regular feature of basic training as the weeks went by.

Ironing uniforms became a common duty — looking good

The first room that I was allocated was with three non-combatants, one of whom was the young fellow from the train trip from South Brisbane. All was going well. Our beds were hospital-taut and the clothing in our lockers all folded in military order, with round edges showing. We were proud of our ability to adapt to the military regimentation, at this level at least.

On the third morning, the corporal swaggered into our room in true military style to announce that I was moving to the next room in exchange for the non-combatant in that room. He gave the impression that the Army wanted them all together and somewhat out of the way. And it had to be done now. All my good work that morning had to be undone, locker contents and bedding, and then re-done next door.

For the remainder of recruit training, I shared the room with Graham Bate, Ivan Standen, both National Servicemen, and some of the time with Jock Hind, a regular volunteer (a 'reg').

Jock was an anomaly, in a world of his own. It was nothing for him to keep us waiting at 0600 hours in the freezing cold of Kapooka while he wandered down the stairs at his own pace. Sometimes he was fully dressed for the day or, on other mornings, the complete opposite, with nothing warm on at all. There were the occasions when he did not turn out at all as he was still in bed, asleep. We were ordered back to our rooms to wait the call to start the day all over again just because Jock did not arrive. I do not remember Jock too much. He lasted just over a couple of weeks before he was discharged as unfit for service.

The author: A well-dressed National Serviceman

Our platoon, 12 Platoon B Company, comprised a mixture of left-over National Servicemen from New South Wales and Queensland

and regular volunteers from all over the country. Graham and I found that we were at least two years older than most of the 'Nashos', and four years older than the regular recruits in out platoon. For me, it was another more belligerent version of the boarding school and clerical life I had experienced previously. I survived the basic training without too many difficult times or injuries, except for briefly being a patient in Wagga Wagga District Hospital.

The routine of being drilled, marched and physically cajoled into being a good soldier continued until the passing-out parade and my appointment to the Australian Services Canteens Organisation (ASCO) for training at Holsworthy Barracks on 1 October 1968.

A DRIVE IN THE COUNTRYSIDE

The Verification

I kept a diary of my time in Vietnam with the Australian Army in 1969. One of the entries there was about a memorable visit to Fire Support and Patrol Base (FSPB) Susan. However, when I spoke to two fellow veterans, Lance Williams and Rodney Hawkins, both of whom had completed two tours with 5 and 7 Battalions, neither had heard of FSPB Susan.

So before I began to write this chapter of my year in Vietnam, I needed to verify that there really was a Fire Support and Patrol Base (FSPB) Susan and that it was where my diary entry said it was. The fact that these experienced infantry men had not heard of FSPB Susan concerned me a great deal. Did I have the name wrong?

Offcuts 2

A fire support base was a fortified position some distance from the 1 Australian Task Force base (1ATF) at Nui Dat in Vietnam, but within artillery range of Nui Dat, to enable wider artillery support for the battalion as they ranged further away from the base. From these bases (and there were many over the ten years), patrols would venture out day and night to disrupt the supply lines of the North Vietnamese Army (NVA) and the Viet Cong.

Many of the Australian FSPBs were named after the various commanders' wives. I am not sure of the implications.

My research led me to a site that named and showed the positions of all the Australian fire support bases that were occupied during Australia's involvement in and around Phuoc Tuy province, Australia's area of operations during the years the Army was in Vietnam. Susan was one of them, with a grid reference YS2864, 1969, the year it was operational. In my acquired collection from my year in Vietnam, I have three maps used by the Australian troops. These and the Google map that also shows the location of Susan corroborated my diary notes.

To further cement the whereabout of FSPB Susan, I read a reference to it in a book entitled *A duty well done: A summary of operations by the Royal Australian Regiment in Vietnam 1965 – 1972*, published in 2011). It showed that FSPB Susan operated during part of my time in the country in 1969. Now I felt confident about writing this chapter.

The Departure

It is 1 June 1969. The previous afternoon, I and Brian Wickes, my fellow worker in the Bulk Store, were ordered to be ready by 0530 hours next day to accompany a convoy going to a fire support base. At that stage, we were not told where we were going. The order was to be ready and waiting down near the fuel depot, which is situated across the road from the PX (shop) and Bulk Store, with SLR (rifle), our one magazine of ammunition and water bottle, at the appointed time.

The order was to wear our long clothing. A good breakfast is ready for us and some others from the Task Force Maintenance Area. We eat quickly, collect our water bottles and rifles — I have one full magazine and the other is always on the SLR, empty — and head to the assembly point.

As we are loaded on to the tray of the empty truck, we are told our destination. We are heading out to Fire Support and Patrol Base, Susan.

FSPB Susan is occupied by a company of 5 Battalion and a troop of 105 Field Battery, a troop of tanks and several Armoured Personal Carriers (APCs), situated at grid reference YS2864. The infantry patrol day and night, keeping the fire support base secure.

On the truck we are also told to reverse our magazines but not to cock the rifles — not real infantry. We are to spend a day outside the protection of the wire of Nui Dat, outside the security of the Task force Base for the first time since being in country.

A sense of adventure, of the unexpected, no fear, a Sunday outing of sorts, but the tension is there. These are the feelings that seem to dominate — something different.

As the convoy assembles, it comprises trucks, mostly empty except for the soldiers from Nui Dat, a couple of Land Rovers for an officer or two, and a number of APCs.

Fire Support and Patrol Base Susan is situated about fifteen miles (24 kms), from Nui Dat, just off the main highway from Long Binh and Saigon. The area skirts the edge of the Mekong Delta. A company of 5 Battalion is being pulled out and returned to Nui Dat for some rest and convalescence and then redeployment to another area of operation. This company has operated from that base for at least three weeks, with the support of a battery of American artillery, a troop of tanks and supporting APCs. They all desperately need a break.

The convoy leaving Nui Dat

We set off, in this large convoy. It is a cloudy, fine day with the sun trying to break through the clouds. We exit the main gate to the Task Force Base towards Baria, the province capital, and then westward along a bitumen main road very needy of repair. I am standing in the back of the truck, with the SLR slung over my shoulder, taking in the most diverse, different landscape that I have ever seen.

There is farming interspersed with fishing and mangroves with the varying odours wafting in the air to help mark the changes. The buildings are clustered in small hamlets or villages and some individually scattered beside the road. People clad in their black pyjamas, the working colour of the peasants, continue about their normal lives as best as they are able, taking little to no interest in the convoy as we drive past.

In my first excursion outside the wire of Nui Dat, I am completely mesmerised with the strange new environment that I find myself being part of. I just balance there in the back of the truck, silently, trying to come to grips with all-new, different, strange sightings: the people, the buildings, the changing smells, the small fields with the people labouring to make a living. They seem so desperate, scratching out an existence on their tiny blocks of land.

The children, in total contrast to the elders, run beside the convoy, calling out and trying to keep pace with the vehicles. This occurs at each village or hamlet. In total contradiction to the state of the housing and the farms in the villages we drive through, I notice a large red church building. It is Catholic in style and design, standing tall and dominating the whole area. It is a total contrast, highlighting that the Christian religion is a significant factor in their lives in this area.

The convoy negotiates quite a few villages when, as we are about to enter another settlement, all the vehicles come without warning to a sudden stop. I wait, expectantly, for a command or even some sort of explosion or just an order to load our SLRs. No direction, no command is passed down the convoy. All vehicles remain stationary while their engines continue to drone away.

I remain standing in the back of the truck in the extreme muggy heat of a Vietnamese summer, the wet season, and wait. Rifles remain uncocked. The breeze of the moving vehicles is not there. Off in the distance, I hear the very distinctive thump, thump, thump of a Huey helicopter approaching the convoy.

It is only then that word filters down to us that a child has run out in front of one of the leading vehicles and was struck. The helicopter was called to airlift the child to receive medical treatment. As the Huey lifts off from a nearby field, the convoy proceeds on its way. I never heard how the child fared.

Soon after, we leave the so-called highway and proceed through very thick scrub.

Turning off the highway towards FSPB Susan

The Arrival

Shortly — I do not remember taking any note of how long it took — a large treeless mound slowly emerges in the distance. The convoy drives through a large cleared area that extends all around the mound. There is a great deal of barren dirt, with little to no distinguishing features. Around the whole area are various layers of barbed wire surrounding the entire mound. Various small pimple-like piles of dirt and sandbag structures are just evident above the barren ground.

It is not until we are very close to the base that the sand bags take the shape of bunkers, barely visible, protruding slightly above the ground. Some tarpaulins provide shade, swelling a little higher above ground level. The tanks and artillery sit in their scrapes, just visible above the ground. Throughout the entire enclosed area, there are soldiers, many shirtless, hustling, moving with a purpose, around and in and out of these partly subterranean structures.

Our presence serves only to intensify the activity throughout the relatively small area that is Fire Support and Patrol Base Susan. When I look more closely around the base, there are several vehicles in addition to the partly concealed artillery, APCs and Centurion tanks. The soldiers manning these vehicles seem to know that they have to wait, knowing they will be the last to move. Nobody, let alone me, seems to care about them at this time. The measured haste of the others in the base is of no concern as they indicate that they know what they are doing.

Soldiers are moving with a purpose, busy going in and out of the bunkers, packing everything, loading the trucks in the convoy with everything that is moveable. Nothing is being left behind.

I have no specific role, no task to undertake, during the packing of the trucks. I just wander around keeping out of harm's way, exploring, all the while keeping an uneasy eye on 'my' truck so it would not leave without me.

I am invited into one bunker that contains men who are just sitting and smoking. The soldiers look as though they are attached to the American unit. These soldiers lounge around, relaxing, smoking, expelling a sweet-smelling smoke, as they await the order to pack up and assemble in the convoy. It is my first experience of smelling the sweet aroma of burning marijuana, pot. They are enjoying a quiet time. I am not offered a joint but I sit and chat.

The final activity is centred around the APCs, the six artillery pieces being connected to vehicles, and the tanks taking their specified defensive position amongst the other vehicles. The armour is the last to be ready to move out after leaving their defensive positions.

The Return Journey

The convoy, re-formed, is much larger than on the trip out. The speed is greatly reduced, much slower than the outward journey, to match that set by the tanks. As we pass back through the villages and hamlets, my thoughts drift, as I stand in the back of the truck, as to what the locals really are thinking about when they see these foreigners roaming around their country warring with and against them. As on the way out, it is the children who take some interest in the convoy with their gestures, friendly or otherwise. Again the adults take little to no interest in the convoy.

The journey back is slow and uneventful. The only compensation is that the heat is dissipating a little.

Brian and I arrive back later in the afternoon after one of the hottest days thus far while being in country, only to find that the others in our unit have just completed concreting the floor in the PX. They are making space for the Hong Kong Concessionaires who are to sell electrical goods and gifts alongside the Australian Forces Canteen Unit (AFCU).

Brian and I express our deep disappointment at not being there to help. The concreters are somewhat sarcastic about the hard day that Brian and I have had riding in the convoy with no ration packs and only our water bottles to keep us going.

Despite their sarcasm, Brian and I are invited to join the concreting group with a few drinks (damaged cans) as we all celebrate their skills as expert concreting tradesmen.

Now that I was back somewhat safe inside the wire, I reflected on the day being vastly different to what I had experienced so far. It was a break in routine and very stimulating in many ways, with a heightened sense of expectation and a sense of potential danger without a feeling of being in danger.

It was during these few beers and while just sitting there, I sensed a feeling of tension, of anxiety that seemed to slowly come to the fore and then began to fade, to drift away. It was replaced with a now-safe feeling, and I relaxed. I came to the realisation that unbeknown to me, throughout the day an amplified sense of tension had existed in me. A sense of wonderment, of potential danger, of the unexpected and, for the first time, the cultural shock as we drove along, had accumulated and stayed with me.

I knew that life had dramatically changed when I'd climbed out of the plane in Saigon just a few weeks earlier, but I now came to know that each new situation brought a new and different normal that I had to adjust to.

As I enjoyed my few cold beers, I relaxed, knowing that I was safer within the wire of Nui Dat.

Vietnam – Peter Darmody

Jim Pascoe

A DAY AT THE PUB

While working for the Brisbane City Council (which I'd joined as an apprentice in 1961), I had been promoted to the position of leading hand 'special class' fitter-mechanic in the Substation Protection section for a number of years. I always found the work diverse and interesting. Our work not only involved that in the Electricity Department, but also carrying out jobs in the Water Supply and Sewerage Department at their pumping stations when the high voltage switchgear required maintenance and the protection and fault monitoring relays were in need of updating. I had worked at both the water supply and sewerage pumping stations and, although they pumped different types of liquid, their operation was of a similar design.

Our section was sometimes requested to carry out work for the private sector as our expertise in the operation and working of the intricate overload and earth leakage protection systems of the network was not available in the general electrical industry.

One such event occurred on Sunday 4 November 1973 when I was tasked to carry out work at the Carlton United Brewery (CUB) in Fortitude Valley. A request was received from CUB for our section to carry out the commissioning checks on their newly installed switchgear which controlled the operation of two new

OFFCUTS 2

Caterpillar diesel alternators. This work was to also include the correct setting up and calibration of the load control relays and associated operation of the tripping current for both thermal, overload and earth leakage systems.

P & P Gold relays were installed to monitor the correct operation of the alternators and I always considered them to be the Rolls Royce of relay protection equipment.

I had an electrical fitter with me and after leaving our depot in Ballow Street, Fortitude Valley, we travelled to the brewery which was close by. Little did we know that it would be some time before we returned to make our way home.

The brewery had organised for a complete shutdown of their operation for the day to enable the new switchgear be commissioned. However, even though there was no power to the site, the company made sure that there was enough sustenance for all.

There were drums filled with ice and tall bottles of Bulimba Bitter inserted in them. No drinkies before commissioning though.

The work progressed well and the foreman and electrical engineer arrived when it was time to commission the alternators. This proved a successful outcome and the alternators were ready for any emergency that might occur in Brisbane.

My foreman, however, then came with a request that, when we had completed the work, there was another job for us. The transformer in the substation at the Piccadilly Arcade in Queen Street had exploded and would have to be replaced. This was something that I wasn't looking forward to as the substation was situated on the third floor of the building and everything had to be manually done with block and tackle.

After finishing at the brewery, we exited from the side door and, as I looked to the South, there was a great green cloud hovering over the Story Bridge. This new job was not looking good. We drove to the Piccadilly Arcade and found that there was no one there so we returned to the depot. It turned out that the Substation Maintenance Branch had been contacted and arrangements were made for their staff to carry out the replacement of the transformer.

What we now also found out was that there were large problems in the electricity network and that every available electrical fitter was required. The cause was a tornado that had its birth at Brookfield, had then travelled through Indooroopilly, and then jumped to Yeronga before finally making landfall at Nathan and destroying the majority of the houses in the vicinity.

As this was a major electrical outage, any staff available were then engaged to try to detect any equipment damage to the electricity network. I accompanied our electrical engineer, Brian Blinco. He would eventually become the General Manager of SEQEB (South East Queensland Electricity Board).

One could say that these were pretty primitive times as two-way radios were not available in many vehicles in the department. In the substations there were telephones which was the only available communication equipment available.

As there was a complete outage (blackout) in the city, it was going to take some time to return supply to the network. There is nothing scarier than driving down Queen Street in complete darkness.

However, looking out over the Story Bridge, was a large illuminated CUB sign for everyone to see. The Carlton Brewery was up and running and the alternators were working perfectly.

We travelled to the yet-to-be commissioned Electricity Department, Control Room, located opposite the Queensland Museum where we gradually brought supply back to the local area.

By now it was approximately 8 pm and, as we'd had lunch at midday, hunger started to come into play. Luckily some biscuits were located in the lunch room and were soon consumed. Arnott's Plain of course.

While patrolling the network in the Brookfield area, where there had been reports of damage, a person covered in bandages and dried blood drove up and said that, if we followed him, we would find where there were wires down. On arrival it was found that this was an understatement. The whole street was completely destroyed. There were wires down everywhere and there would be no restoration of supply until these repairs were effected.

The next job was to follow the 11,000 volt overhead feeder wires that supplied power to the extremity of the Brookfield area and to check for any further damage that had not already been reported. Have you ever traipsed through heavy scrub in the middle of the night looking for downed overhead wires?

The method was to leap frog the poles. I would walk from one pole to the next and Brian would go from there to the next. I would then drive to the next one. It was a long night but eventually supply was restored and we were able to return to the depot.

Since starting work at the brewery, we had been working continuously for twenty-four hours and, after picking up our vehicles we headed for home. It was time for a nice long sleep.

After a great night's rest, it was back to work at the Colmslie substation, where a tick was detected lodged in my neck. This was the aftermath of the night trek through the scrub. It was removed via a pair of pliers. What would 'Health and Safety' say about that today?

Following the tornado, there was a large amount of work required to restore supply back to normal but this was of no concern to our section.

A few weeks after the tornado event, our engineer informed me that he had received an invitation from the Carton United Brewery for us to attend an executive meeting at their Fortitude Valley premises. It turned out that this was in appreciation of the work that had been done in restoring supply to their business. Who would have believed that the commissioning of their alternators could have come at a more appropriate time?

I was fortunate enough to be invited to attend another function at the brewery after the 1974 floods and that was in appreciation for restoring supply to the electrical distribution system and getting their hotels operating again.

Offcuts 2

AN OCEAN VOYAGE

In 1966 I was a member of the Royal Australian Naval Reserve and based at HMAS *Moreton* in New Farm, Brisbane. The reserves, as we were known, had the job of supplying the initial set-up of stores and equipment for top-secret missile-firing trials off Fairfax Island, off the central Queensland coast, and to bring all surplus equipment back to Brisbane on completion. I was part of the crew for the support trip.

The Ikara missile (meaning *throwing stick*) was an Australian-designed rocket propelled anti-submarine torpedo, developed in the mid-1960s. It was fitted to the Torrens Class frigates and Adelaide Class destroyers. HMAS *Stuart* was the trials ship and she had a team of clearance divers on board and was also assisted by the boom defence vessel HMAS *Kimbla*.

The Fairfax Islands were a pair of cays and part of the Bunker Group, situated 113 kilometres east of Gladstone and 405 kilometres north of Brisbane. They are now part of the Barrier Reef National Park. These two cays were surrounded by a reef and separated by a large lagoon. The north cay was barren and covered in bomb and artillery craters and inhabited by goats and rats. The south cay was covered in shrubbery and had a long sand spit extending to the south and this is where a large aerial was erected. There was a Nissan hut here housing the scientists from the Aeronautical Research Laboratories who were located there during the trials that were carried out over a number of months.

Her Majesty's Australian Motor Refrigeration Lighter (MRL) 253 was the training ship for the Brisbane Division and used for these trips. She was a World War II motor-refrigerated lighter and had been based at HMAS *Terangau* on Manus Island until returning to Australia. It was sent to Brisbane to replace the general supply vessel GPV 957, another old WW II craft that had failed to pass survey. She initially rated two refrigerated holds and a compressor compartment situated on the main deck between them. The refrigerant coils were removed from the holds as were the compressors from the ice house. The ice house, as it was called, was reconfigured into crew accommodation and equipped with hammocks. This was my crew space for the trip. Our crew was made up of approximately 18 reservists from Brisbane, Sydney, Melbourne and Adelaide of whom three were officers. All of us were undertaking the obligatory 13-day annual continuous training period.

Being top secret trials, a security briefing was given where we were informed that cameras were not to be taken.

After loading stores, we cast off and headed down the Brisbane River and, after we checked the compass at the Hamilton Swing Basin, MRL 253 proceeded out into Moreton Bay. As the electrical mechanic, I was classed as special sea duty man and had to stand by in the bow just in case the anchor had to be dropped.

It was a leisurely cruise until the open sea was reached. Then it became a different matter with waves breaking over the bow and sweeping down the deck. Getting to our mess deck was an adventure, a slightly damp one. In the wheelhouse, it wasn't much better and the sub-lieutenant would come on watch with his own bucket. Oh well, it happens to everyone. Being a small craft, all the crew took a turn at the wheel or being on lookout duty.

HMA Motor Refrigeration Lighter (MRL) 253

It was a leisurely two-day cruise with activities of rifle and pistol shooting on the way. There were eight hundred rounds of rifle and three hundred rounds of pistol ammunition to be expended on the trip.

Fairfax Island was eventually reached and the *Stuart* and *Kimbla* were there finalising the trials. A lattice target on a raft was towed by *Kimbla* to the test area and then returned at night. There was also a fleet air arm Iroquois helicopter in use and based at Bundaberg during the trials and flown out to the island every day.

For a few days there was nothing to do. Time was spent fishing, exploring the cays and walking around the reef checking the coral. Some of the more colourful ones were brought back to our mess. This was fine for a few days until we experienced a terrible smell and found that it came from the dying coral. It was immediately thrown overboard.

One of our crew came in contact with some coral that cut his ankle causing coral poisoning. He had to be taken by helicopter to Bundaberg for treatment.

One morning, the captain asked the cook if fish could be put on the menu. The clearance divers were contacted and they detonated some explosives in the lagoon where there were schools of trevally swimming around. The result of this was that we had a fridge full of fish which the skipper alone filleted before being cooked by our chef.

Night fishing was taken up by all the crew and one of them caught a large mackerel. Being the largest fish caught to that point, the banned cameras were brought out to record this event. However no one had a flash gun. I believe that there aren't many times a forty kilowatt generator is brought 'on line' to provide supply to a twenty-inch signalling lamp for that purpose.

Every night an anchor and security watch was kept and it was amazing to see the large number of fish, turtles, sea snakes and huge sharks swimming around our vessel. The sea turtles would come ashore at night and lay their eggs on the sand spit.

Eventually word was given that the stores could at last be embarked. This was done by way of using the helicopter to bring the equipment from shore and lowering it by cargo net onto a 20-metre raft which was then brought alongside and the gear winched inboard and stored in the two holds.

One time the helicopter crew were lowering the net, and two of our crew, who were manning the raft, grasped the net for positioning when all of a sudden the helicopter rose up and moved slightly away. The raft crew held onto the net until they let go and hit the water. This was the day after a large shark had been sighted nearby. To this day, I swear that both of the crew ran on the water back to the raft.

Some equipment was not to be returned and so was dumped outside the reef. The same fate awaited the large mast on the sand spit. The Nissan hut being used by the scientists was supposed to have been burned down but the captain received permission to have it left for emergency purposes.

One cargo net load comprised two acetylene bottles which fell out during lowering and disappeared into the water. Years later some recreational divers found some torpedoes off shore and the emergency services and water police were involved in recovering them. I always wondered if they were the lost gas bottles.

Eventually we sailed from Fairfax Island and made our way to Bundaberg. We tied up there at the sugar wharf for a couple of days before casting off and sailing through Hervey Bay out through the waters at Inskip Point before making for Brisbane.

It was a beautiful fine day as we proceeded down the coast and the surplus flares and rockets were expended on the way until Moreton Bay was reached at sundown. Proceeding up the Brisbane River, we were challenged by the Bishop Island signal station. As luck would have it, the circuit supplying the aldis lamp was faulty and once again the generator was 'flashed up' and the large signal lamp used to reply to the request. I would not have liked to have been on the receiving end of that light.

We berthed at HMAS *Moreton* at 11 pm and the last job for the night was to inform Navy Office in Sydney of our safe arrival.

It took two more days to de-store and pack the equipment to be returned to the research department. Then it was farewell to everyone. Our captain, a lieutenant commander, was a very well-liked member of the crew, and we presented him with a Pisonia tree in a pot before leaving the island. He brought it back with him to Brisbane and then had the plant sent home to Sydney with one of the crew.

Skipper of MRL 253 with his gift of a Pisonia plant

It was a great trip and a never forgotten holiday. The other good part was that the Brisbane City Council paid me for my two weeks away in addition to my pay from the Navy. This was only a few months before I was to be married and so the extra money certainly came in handy.

Offcuts 2

WORKING IN THE 1974 BRISBANE FLOODS

I received a phone call just after breakfast on Saturday, 26 January 1974. It was my Substation Protection section foreman asking me if I was available to carry out work in restoring supply to premises around Brisbane. The Control Centre was inundated with requests for assistance from consumers, and their staff were fully engaged.

It had been raining for three weeks and now cyclone *Wanda* (which hardly rated as a cyclone) decided to dump more rain across an already saturated Queensland. All the dams were full to capacity and water was pouring over spillways and making their way into the Brisbane River catchment area. Wivenhoe Dam had not been constructed then.

On arrival, I was given another electrical fitter as my assistant and we made our way to the Control Centre at Albert Park. A number of jobs were allocated to us and, after filling our van with a wide variety of fuses, we set off.

Sometimes we were lucky and it only required a fuse wire replacement but other times it was a matter of getting out the ladder and climbing a pole to replace a primary fuse. When we had completed the work given, we went back for more. There were not many two-way radios in those days.

A loss-of-supply job was given for the Park Royal Hotel in Alice Street, Brisbane. On arrival, nothing could be done to restore supply as the rainwater had come in and, seeping through the besser brick walls, had penetrated the main switchboard, causing massive damage. The floor in the area was covered in water and oil which had come from the kitchen.

Another job we attended was at premises in Butterfield Street, Herston. When looking at a flooded Breakfast Creek, all we could see were hundreds of packets of Panda potato chips as well as bottles of cordial floating past. These had been washed away from the Mynor factory which was located nearby. I loved Panda potato chips. What a waste.

We were working in the Northwest area as the sun set but there was no let-up of work. The next job was at some flats where one tenant had lost supply. The tenant next door asked us if we could see him after we had restored supply. We found out that he had cooked us a meal of curried mince. Never were we so thankful because all we had eaten were some biscuits as everything was shut.

We arrived home at about 11 pm that night and, after a very good night's sleep it was back at the depot for a 7.30 am start next day.

The flood waters on Sunday had begun to rise. The job for the day was to drive to the Fairfield substation and prepare for the total disconnection of supply as it was in a low-lying area where waters were coming up.

After parking our vehicles on high ground, we rowed over to the substation in an aluminium dinghy. Then the four of us waited and watched the water slowly rising until word was given to carry out some switching in the 33,000 volt switch yard. I don't think that I will ever see switching being performed from a dinghy again.

The substation was still energised and we watched the water rise over the floor and then become level with the water from the toilet bowl. It was time to leave but not before all the load control relays were removed. It was fortunate that this substation was of a relatively new design and the relays were of a type that they could be racked from their cases. A few trips were needed to carry them to safety before we finally returned to our base and then made our way home again.

Fairfield substation switchyard

I hadn't had much time to speak with my heavily pregnant wife Janice since the previous Friday night. She had spent most of the time at home with our two young children.

On arrival at work next morning, the foreman informed me that I was to leave my vehicle in the depot and take my van and work from home. I didn't see my car for another week.

By this time Oxley was being inundated by flood waters and the Oxley substation was being prepared for decommissioning. The entire area would be totally without supply until further notice.

The local service station, run by 'Snow' Hunter in Oxley Road near Bayford Street was where Alderman Gordon Thompson had set up his office as an emergency hub. I informed him that supply would be soon switched off until further notice. He soon got rid of all the nuisances by telling them what was about to happen.

Fairfield substation

There were four other electrical fitters at the Oxley substation and, when they eventually disconnected supply, they found that they couldn't return home as all access roads were flooded. That night, we had four extra people in our house. Breakfast next day consisted of bread and butter and black tea before they were able to make their way home.

For the next week I worked from home. I was the only substation fitter on the Oxley side of the Walter Taylor bridge, together with a truck driver and an overhead linesman who both lived at Inala.

We were luckier than other residents as our street was supplied with electricity from the Darra substation. There's nothing like living on a hill and hearing the flood water roaring back into Ralph Brittain's Bricks clay pit. It was to take him many weeks to pump out this water before he could again make bricks.

OFFCUTS 2

I had my camera with me during this time and a number of flood photos were taken in black and white format. My foreman took the film to the BCC photographer who had them developed for our section as there were no other photos taken.

Following the floods, I was eventually able to retrieve my car from the depot and return it to its rightful owner, my wife Janice.

It was a very interesting time and our department made a number of inventions that enabled us to restore our equipment back into operation. Eventually, a number of flying gangs were formed and consisted of two Substation Protection and two Maintenance fitters. These went into the substations and brought everything back to a workable state before commissioning back into the electrical network.

Yacht – Alan Smith

Trevor Ross Armstrong

A HITCHHIKER'S GUIDE TO TRAVELLING TO OTHER INTERESTING PLACES

I used to walk, or ride ponies or pushbikes where I wished to go or muster on our Seven-Mile Creek to Ebenezer dairy/beef farm. It's also how I used to travel to and from Rosewood State School in the 1950s.

When our family moved to our new Ipswich home, I replaced ponies with public transport, but had to walk or ride to Ipswich Railway stations to catch passenger trains or buses. But after having my *Malvern Star* bicycle stolen and needing to travel regularly to and from Indooroopilly or Toowong stations to the University of Queensland at St Lucia (where I was attending lectures for my B. Agr. Sc. Degree), I resorted to hitchhiking from 1966.

Along with other students, before we had access to our own motor vehicles or motor bikes, hitchhiking became a convenient, cheap and safe method of transport. Even though warned of unsavoury drivers/characters, I never encountered any, but on a crowded evening train on my way home to Ipswich, I was once molested by a sneaky homosexual under his *Telegraph* newspaper.

In May 1968, the Australasian Association of Agricultural Faculties conference was being held in Perth. I was determined to participate by hitchhiking along the Cunningham Highway from

Amberley, near our farm, to cross the border at Goondiwindi into NSW, down the Newell Highway through Moree to Dubbo, across the Hay Plain and Darling River to Broken Hill. My scout's sleeping bag did not keep me warm enough on top of a roadside bulldozer bonnet, so I paid for meals, rooms and showers in country pubs on the way.

Road maps showed short cuts across the South Australian border to Port Augusta at the top of Spencer's Gulf. So I enjoyed an early breakfast at another roadhouse truck stop where I was prepared to bargain with truckies who wanted a companion willing to keep them awake while they were driving, and wake them up after short cat naps. Ceduna at the top of the Great Australian Bight was then the end of the bitumen on the Eyre Highway and the start for the longest, wettest and boggiest detours around already bogged B-doubles and other vehicles and caravans. So while I ate I arranged with roadhouse proprietors that I was willing to pay alternate fuel fills for anyone willing to take me right across the notorious Nullarbor Plain. But my agreed driver turned out to be a disturbed delinquent running away from home in a suspect vehicle.

My final driver, from Kalgoorlie to Perth, was a non-talkative gold digger with two lovely daughters, the eldest of whom had been severely burnt and scarred and was embarrassingly shy. As I had lectures starting soon after this successful conference ended, I flew to Sydney, trained it to Windsor, and hitchhiked home via the New England Highway. By now I'd learnt how to give potential picker-uppers the best chances for seeing, assessing, stopping and safely allowing me to stow my back-pack and clamber on board.

I gradually lost my original first love, but gained other girl friends from these ventures. My fellow 'Agies' dubbed me *Charmstrong* in our Ag Students Magazine for my antics of asking charming, interesting girls for their contact details e.g. name, address or phone number (before modern electronic communications) for future, potential and enjoyable mutual liaisons.

HELPING MANAGE OUR LOCAL NATURAL ENVIRONMENT

I first encountered a group of kids from Eden Academy Early Learning, Corinda by chance in May 2021 when they were being ably led by Miss Janet on a walking excursion through our local George Scarlett Park. I asked her if the kids would be interested in experiencing neighbouring Pennywort Creek rehabilitation and she said yes.

We diverted temporarily to watch EcoServices' contractor William demonstrate and explain using his narrow spade to dig, place water gel and fertilizer tablets in a hole before taking a native basket grass (*Lomandra longifolia*) tubeling from his pouch, tickling its bottom roots and planting it deeply while padding down damp soil around it.

Preferably each planting would receive a hardwood stake driven into its upstream side to help protect it from flood debris and a tree guard if it was likely to be disturbed by brush turkeys or other creatures.

Post planting as well as regular watering and weeding are necessary parts of an integrated management program, even if coir matting and/or bark mulching are included to aid successful establishment and avoid losses of moisture, plants and soil by erosion.

Even the younger children in the group were keen observers. So Miss Janet asked if I would be willing to continue sharing our environmental education by coming to the Academy a couple of weeks later.

At that session, I gave a presentation on how we can all help manage our local natural environment by understanding the carbon cycle: carbon and nutrients in the soil can be converted by multitudes of microorganisms, water and sunlight via seeds germinating, growing and producing plant foods for animals, including us, to eat and/or use as fibres for clothes, shelter etc.

We can prepare suitable land areas by controlling weeds and planting desirable herbs, shrubs and trees and continually tending these until they are ready for harvesting or conserving as habitat for native animals.

For example, we can water and germinate flower or vegetable crops before planting in our home gardens or plant silky oak tubelings in local bushland habitats for future harvesting and preparing to make beautiful furniture.

Reusing, repurposing or recycling useful items is desirable, especially through Containers For Change which pays 10 cents per aluminium can, glass and plastic drink bottles. Collection can be assisted with a special pick-up tool. Also, we need to avoid littering, especially elastic bands, metal rings or other items likely to strangle or choke native animals and birds.

FLOOD EXPERIENCES

I remember as a child viewing pictures in books depicting frightened families caught on furniture surrounded by rising, expansive flood waters. Dad was aware that our '7-Mile' Dairy Farm flooded. He'd bought this bare, potential cultivation for cropping in a rural area outside Ipswich when he turned 21 in 1928. His father had witnessed the highest 1893 and other floods from his adjacent home on *Springhill*, Ebenezer.

My first experiences of floods were in the wet 1950s when I was living with my parents and siblings on this adjacent farm. Our high-set home overlooked an alluvial black soil flood plain of the Bremer River which bent from its south-west source of the Great Dividing Range, near Rosevale to the north-east at the Seven Mile Bridge leading towards Ipswich.

Heavy rain in the Bremer catchment led to flood waters overflowing its banks with increasingly fast-flowing dirty waters. Various levels of flood rubbish became visible as the water eroded previously deposited silt and turned it into soggy mud. Stock were bogged and so were us kids if we sank over our knees.

We were warned never to play in our deep, water-filled silo between our farm buildings, or in the large river holes, unless supervised by our older siblings. They could swim, having had swimming lessons. This was in contrast to the novice dog-paddling of my twin sister, pet Kelpie cattle dog and me. We splashed close to two levels of saplings and wires strung around local creek trees, allowing crossings when floods covered our farm bridges. We used this crossing if our milking cows were caught by flash flooding on the other side of the creek — necessitating our coaching them to swim back for twice daily milking.

Dad had a daily fresh milk run to Ipswich families, so when flooding threatened our normal roads, he would check our closest Bremer River levels about one kilometre south of where Mum was milking cows in bails before deciding if he could drive via the Seven Mile Bridge or other flood diversion routes. The maximum flood height on the Seven Mile Bridge gauge that would allow our loaded Army Austin or Holden Ute to cross safely was 18 inches. If there was any doubt of wash-outs or bridge damage, Dad would wade in and check surfaces before venturing through fast-flowing floods.

When waters were only slightly too high, Mum could approve one or more of us kids to accompany Dad via the top Bremer Bridge on Mt Walker Road and then via unsealed Ebenezer Road. On one occasion, we bogged to the chassis where the Moreton Shire Council had graded dirt to become deep mud over a gully crossing. Dad had to walk through forested country to a neighbour to arrange for his tractor and chain to pull us through to the bitumen. Extra hands helped dad catch up delivering fresh milk to his customers before their breakfasts.

Higher, prolonged floods necessitated longer detours, via Tallegalla and Marburg if there'd been only local recent heavy rains, or via Minden if there was higher gully and more widespread flooding. Dad only missed the odd milk run delivery from the 1930s depression to the 1965 prolonged drought, when he sold our fresh milk run and we switched to contract cream and milk cans/tanker collections for delivery to the Booval Butter Factory. By then we had more reliable electricity connections over the more frequently flooding Bremer River, raised new bails and later a herring bone dairy with milk chilling and cold room facilities plus a covered cow yard over coal-based foundations.

Flood experiences of 1974 required droving all stock from this 7-Mile dairy farm up across the rail line in Rosewood to the family farm of the wife of my brother Roy. They were herded up to *Perry's Knob* for a few days subsistence, until it was safe to return. It took months for the stock, land and farm business to recover, but with persistent work by many helpers over the following seasons, the farm gradually recovered and the extended family grew, with new higher areas purchased.

Our descendants saved valuable cattle in the 2022 floods. Subsequently, however, these same prime, fat stock, ready to sell, slowly died from what autopsies by a veterinarian revealed was a mystery wasting lantana-like poisoning disease or pneumonia complex.

PENNYWORT CREEK HISTORY AND REHABILITATION

For tens of thousands of years, the catchment east of the 15-mile reach of the current Brisbane River — from Keble Street, Corinda to Oxley Creek via the south east of Cliveden Avenue's Oxley Golf Complex — has formed a watercourse that today is known as Pennywort Creek. This God's/local *Yugera* Indigenous people's country would have been traversed, utilised, lived on and managed for its native vegetation, land and water natural resources in their own hunter and gatherer ways.

When European explorers, settlers and farmers arrived from the mid-1800s, they tended to clear competing weeds to graze and grow pastures, vegetables and other crops. The richer alluvial soils, without complete vegetation cover along the flood plain, tended to erode when inevitable flash flooding occurred.

Pennywort Creek flooding early 2022

The earliest aerial photo of Pennywort Creek, taken in 1937, shows its sparse vegetation, with a much more meandering course of slower flowing, less eroding nature than currently occurs. Today there is more run-off from hard surfaces of roads, roofs, school tennis courts and the like. So Oxley Creek Catchment Association (OCCA), Brisbane City Council's Habitat Brisbane and other partnerships encourage volunteers through CreekCare, CreekWatch, and local BushCare Groups to form, prepare and plant local trees, shrubs and ground covers to better manage these threatening environmental issues.

Shield Pennywort (*Hydrocotyl verticillata*) occurs in Queensland and New South Wales, but nowhere is it widespread. Records show it was found in 1875 at a location given only as 'Brisbane

River'. However, the only place this is currently known to grow in the Brisbane area is at Pennywort Creek. It is important to protect Shield Pennywort and its habitat, and under State legislation it cannot be collected.

Pennywort CreekCare group planting native trees near Oxley Golf Complex

In 2003, Cliveden Avenue Reserve BushCare Group, led by Carole Bristow, took on restoration of a section of this creek. From 2006, OCCA advocated for naming it Pennywort Creek and was successful in 2008. A separate Pennywort Creek BushCare Group was formed under Habitat Brisbane, led by David Sparks until I was appointed as Group Leader.

The endangered Angle-stemmed Myrtle (*Gossia gonaclada*) is also present along with about 80 other native plants, helping form a habitat corridor for many animals like the Rakali (Native Water Rat).

Under the Pennywort Creek BushCare Site Plan (2020) progress is being made in 2022, with restoration and rehabilitation extending south and west with the cooperation of Corinda State Primary School teachers, students and others.

Sketches and Stories From the Shed

Drongo – Anthony Durrington

DARRYL DYMOCK

WHITE CHALK AND JUNIPER GREEN: TEACHING WITH THE ARMY IN PNG[1]

In August 1966, 25 young Australian soldiers landed at Jackson's Strip airport Port Moresby, in what was then the Territory of Papua and New Guinea,[2] with with only a hazy idea of why they were there.

These young men were all school teachers, and they'd been conscripted into the Australian Army. Although they didn't know it at the time, this group of 25 was the vanguard of a taskforce of some 300 conscripted teachers sent to PNG between 1966 and 1972.

Under the National Service scheme introduced by the Menzies Government in 1965, all 20-year-old males had to register for National Service, commonly known as 'Nasho'. Between 1965 and 1972 almost 64,000 of these young men were randomly selected in a subsequent birthday ballot to serve in the Australian Army for two years (reduced to 18 months in 1971-2).

---

1 An earlier version of this story was published online by Military History Heritage Victoria.

2 In this article, 'PNG' is sometimes used for ease of reference, although officially TPNG did not become Papua New Guinea until 1971. The country became self-governing in 1974 and gained independence in 1975.

From 1966, about a quarter of these conscripts were sent to fight alongside regular soldiers in Vietnam, where Australia and other nations were supporting the US against feared communist expansion in south-east Asia. Some 200 Nashos died there.

While the focus was on Vietnam, senior officers in the Army seized on the opportunity of National Service to meet a need they had earlier identified elsewhere: improving the educational levels of the 2500 indigenous soldiers in TPNG, who at that time were part of the Australian Army.

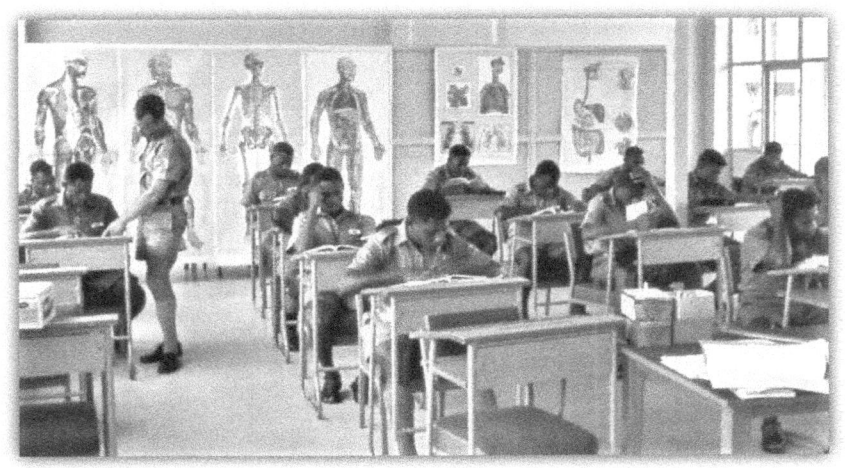

A Chalkie sergeant teaching troops of Pacific Islands Regiment, PNG

In particular, Brigadier Ian Hunter, Head of PNG Command, and Brigadier Maurice 'Bunny' Austin, Deputy Adjutant-General in Canberra, regarded such a development as vital for the growth and stability of a country they saw as heading towards self-government and independence sooner rather than later. This was not the official government view at the time.

These two visionaries realised that National Service was bringing substantial numbers of trained teachers into the Army, and they decided to make use of that expertise in TPNG.

I know about this venture because, in 1969–70, I was one of those 300 conscripted teachers, colloquially known as 'Chalkies'. After recruit training at Singleton in NSW and a short education posting in Brisbane, I was sent to Taurama Barracks near Port Moresby for twelve months from late 1969. Fortunately my wife Cheryl was soon able to join me (and our first child was born there in April 1970).

The author: Education Sergeant in PNG 1970

Between 1966 and 1973, tours of duty in PNG ranged from 12 to 18 months. By the time I arrived there for my 12-month stint, the Army was posting about 40 conscripted teachers a year to PNG Command. The early cohorts of Chalkies were plucked from other Corps such as Ordnance and Artillery, and reposted with little notice to the Royal Australian Army Educational Corps.

Later, incoming teachers were invited during the recruit training phase to *apply* for selection in Education, rather than being snatched seemingly indiscriminately from other corps. In all, only a small proportion of incoming Nasho teachers were selected for Education, however.

Some of us chosen for the Educational Corps had taught in primary or secondary schools for a year prior to Nasho; others came direct from teachers college or university. The criteria for selection weren't clear, although the ability to mix with 'non-whites' and/or to play sport appeared to be important.

Education has a long history in the Australian Army and there was already a handful of full-time officers serving in TPNG. The newly posted Nasho teachers overnight were promoted from private to sergeant, a move understandably not always welcomed by regular NCOs who had taken years to rise through the ranks. In PNG we also adopted the juniper green uniforms of the Pacific Islands Regiment.

After passing through the brick wall of humidity at Jackson's Strip airport in Moresby, each annual Chalkie cohort was divided among the five Army bases in the Territory: HQ at Murray Barracks, 1st Pacific Islands Regiment (1 PIR) at nearby Taurama Barracks, the Recruit Training Depot at Goldie River (30 km from Moresby), Igam Barracks at Lae on the North Coast, and 2 PIR at Moem Barracks near Wewak, on the north-west coast. 2PIR also serviced an outpost at Vanimo on the border with Indonesian West Irian (now West Papua).

There was also an agricultural adviser posting ('didiman' in Pidgin) at Moem Barracks, and a couple of Chalkies were seconded to Iduabada Technical College in Port Moresby.

When we reached our new postings, we quickly found ourselves in the classroom — teaching English, Maths, Social Studies and Science, creating pathways to educational certificates. Importantly, we also discussed the role of an army in a democracy. Classes were fitted around the troops' military training commitments.

Most Chalkies were single and so lived and ate in the Sergeants' Mess. Early arrivals were surprised to find themselves housed in tents, and teaching in makeshift classrooms; later Education sergeants were fortunate to live and work in modern purpose-built facilities. The few married Chalkies were usually fortunate to be allocated a house on the base we were posted to.

In hindsight, the Army had high expectations of the 300 or so Nasho Chalkies sent to PNG over those eight years. Few of us were aware at the time of the potential contribution we might be making to the future development of an emerging Pacific nation.

Individually, however, we readily accepted the responsibility and unexpected professional autonomy, often developing our own resources. We were glad to be able to make use of our teacher training, although this was within a pervasive military context that some conscripted Chalkies understandably found constraining and frustrating.

As sergeants we also had military duties on the bases where we served; some Chalkies accompanied the troops on civic action patrols around the country, and also joined or coached their sporting teams, and showed movies in the Mess. After hours we made our own fun, some buying cars or motor-bikes and audio equipment, or taking advantage of cross-country charter flights.

After completing their two years National Service, many Chalkies returned to the education systems they'd come from in Australia and resumed their disrupted civilian lives. Others moved into different careers, from real estate to the diplomatic service, and a few, like me, found their way back to PNG to make a further contribution.

The overall significance of our potential contribution to PNG dawned slowly. It was several decades later, early in the 21st century, that Chalkies began to meet and talk at reunions across Australia, to publish memoirs and establish a website.

Those initiatives gave some of us an opportunity to rediscover the time we'd spent in the Army in PNG as fresh-faced 20-somethings. It was a chance to reflect on its possible significance for that nation's development, as well as its impact on our own personal and professional lives.

I was spurred to write a book about our experiences, *The Chalkies: Educating an army for independence*, based on a survey of more than 70 of those 300 Nashos posted to PNG between 1966 and 1973.

In early 2022 the State Library of Queensland acknowledged the role the Chalkies played in PNG through a series of video interviews that I helped facilitate. Those interviews are available through the library's catalogue, as part of its military history collection.

The author at presentation of Chalkies video interviews for State Library of Queensland 2022

The Education scheme in PNG between 1966 and 1973 was a product of its time, taking advantage of a process of conscription established for a military purpose, and diverting a cohort of teachers for an educational role with the army of a 'country' on its way to independence. Not all Chalkies were convinced they made a lasting impact, but there was general agreement that if we had to be in the Army, teaching in PNG at least made use of the profession we'd been trained in.

In my own case, the experience of teaching adults in PNG changed my career trajectory from high school teaching — initially I returned there as a civilian college lecturer (where I saw the birth of an independent PNG), followed by postgraduate studies leading to academic appointments at several Australian universities; and satisfying opportunities to continue to use and share my knowledge and skills into older age.

A LIFETIME OF LEARNING AND A LOVE OF WORDS[3]

My role as convenor of the motley mob known as the Writers Group at Oxley Men's Shed came about through my own interest in writing stories and helping others do the same.

My writing journey began in 2005 when I decided I'd 'retire' from full-time employment and try to balance my working life between income-earning activities of my own choosing and writing a book, or at least a short story or two, with the aim of publication. (Income from publication was a distant hope rather than a strategy!)

The twists and turns of that journey have not only helped me develop my writing, but have provided me with fascinating and helpful insights into the world of publishing.

I have of course been writing and publishing in my academic work for many years. I've researched, written and co-edited books and numerous journal articles and book chapters. In recent years these have been mostly on aspects of adult and workplace learning and vocational education and training.

Writing outside my academic area for a wider audience was a new challenge.

To kickstart my 'professional' writing career, in 2006 I enrolled in a year-long course on fiction writing with the Queensland Writers Centre (QWC) followed by another year-long course on editing my novel. The result was my first narrative *non-fiction* book!

---

3 An expanded version of this article was published in the newsletter of the Australian Council for Adult Literacy.

The process began when a chance comment sparked my interest in researching the life of Bundaberg-born Bert Hinkler, a national hero and world-wide sensation when he made the first solo flight from England to Australia in an open-cockpit plane in 1928.

Unfortunately there was already a published biography of Hinkler. So I decided I'd aim at the young adult market by weaving a fiction story of a teenager who travelled back in time and met the famous aviator and tried to change his future. Hence my novel-writing course.

Those courses opened my eyes to my own limitations as well as publishers' expectations of writers. I learnt a lot from an exceptional tutor, author Kim Wilkins.

Shortly afterwards, I had the opportunity at a writers festival to show the draft of my young adult novel to a literary agent. Encouragingly, she thought the manuscript was worth another look, but then said, 'Why don't you write a non-fiction book about Hinkler?'

'Because there's already another biography. Published 1962.'

'Could be time for another one,' she said.

And she was right. In 2010, my draft narrative non-fiction biography of Bert Hinkler was selected for the Hachette Australia/ Queensland Writers Centre manuscript development program. Three years later, after a few more twists and turns, blood, sweat and tears, Hachette Australia published *Hustling Hinkler: the tumultuous life of a trailblazing Australian aviator.*

Hustling Hinkler *was published in 2013, reprinted 2022*

Along the way, I gained more insights into the publishing industry, including the challenges of working with a professional editor and the value of having a book promoted and distributed nationally. *Hustling Hinkler* was launched at Riverbend Books, Bulimba in 2013.

I was also thrown into the world of media interviews and public talks. At one Brisbane suburban library a man in the audience not only told us he'd been a toddler on his father's shoulders when Bert Hinkler flew into Bundaberg in 1928, but launched into one of the popular songs of the time: 'Hustling Hinkler, up in the sky...'. He knew all the words, and we warmly applauded his effort.

Frustratingly, another author and publisher had also decided it was time for a new biography of Bert Hinkler. It took 18 months for my version to appear, and their book appeared on the shelves first. Nevertheless, *Hustling Hinkler* sold quite well, and in 2022 Hachette Australia announced a reprint.

While I waited, I was working on another book and also continued to teach and research part-time at Griffith University. I was intrigued that some people, like me, were continuing to work beyond traditional retiring age, while others were leaving paid work relatively early, some apparently unaware of how much longer we're now generally living. Hence the book *Extending your use-by date*.

One of the intriguing aspects of that book's journey was that after some interest from traditional publishers it was picked up by an e-publisher, Xoum (now Brio). My agent at the time told me I was probably the only person in Australia who had a print book (*Hustling Hinkler*) and an e-book published in the same year.

Extending your use-by date generated a lot of media interest. I found myself doing radio interviews with presenters across Australia, including several from the 'Tardis', the solo booth in ABC's Brisbane studio. Channel 9's Lisa Wilkinson interviewed me for the *Today* show. In 2014, Xoum published a print version. Despite the publicity, the book didn't sell well enough to make my fortune, but I learnt a lot about how the media operates.

Two years later, my experience as an educator and a researcher came together for my next book. Based on a survey of over 70 former members of the Royal Australian Army Educational Corps, *The Chalkies* (Australian Scholarly Publishing 2016) tells the story of the 300 conscripted teachers sent to Papua New Guinea between 1966 and 1973 to raise the educational levels of Pacific Islander troops. I was one of those conscripts, a reluctant National Servicemen for two years, but glad that I could utilise the teaching skills I'd learnt before I was called up.

The draft of that young adult novel I wrote with the QWC in the mid-2000s is still in my desk drawer. Despite my focus on non-fiction books, however, I still like the challenge of fiction writing.

In non-fiction, you have to get the story as right as you can, and not stray outside the storyline. Even if you're being creative with some aspects, the basic facts have to be correct and the people and situations real. Fiction on the other hand allows you to create characters and scenarios and develop a story of your own choosing that you hope others will want to read.

I decided early in my new writing life that I'd try my hand at short fiction. Competitions seemed a good way to go — they have a word limit and a deadline to work to, and I'd be testing myself against the field.

After a slow start, the results have been encouraging. My first success (after two years of trying) was a story selected for one of the annual anthologies *One Book Many Brisbanes*, sponsored in more arty times by the Brisbane City Council.

Since then I've had short fiction published in other anthologies, including the 2019 Margaret River Short Story competition. My most significant fiction achievement to date is winning the 2016 Roly Sussex Short Story award, which was presented to me by the Queensland Governor.

Of course, I've submitted other short fiction stories that didn't make the cut. Nevertheless, the occasional successes in competitions have helped encourage me along my writing journey, especially when I've been labouring for some time trying to wrangle a non-fiction manuscript into shape.

They've shown me that there are times when I can rise above the rest in my writing and convinced me that while I might never make the best seller list, I do have some talent.

There is some overlap in that my fiction stories are mostly based on my non-fiction research. For example, the *One Book Many Brisbanes'* story was woven around a newspaper item about Bert Hinkler that I came across while researching for his biography.

That research also tossed up the name of another early Australian aviator, Harry Hawker. I knew nothing about him, but discovered that he too was famous in his day. Probably most intriguing, however, is that although Harry Hawker and Bert Hinkler were born around the same time and had similar childhood backgrounds (in different states), their lives strongly diverged when they moved to England before World War I to pursue aviation careers. Regrettably, however, they also shared the tragedy of an early death in a solo plane crash.

So, over several years, in the midst of university teaching and research and other writing endeavours, I explored Harry Hawker's story. The result was *A Great and Restless Spirit: the incredible true story of Harry Hawker*, published in 2022 (Armour Books).

A Great and Restless Spirit *was published in 2022*

In that book I've tried to focus not only on Hawker's achievements, but also his personal characteristics and especially the role of his English-born wife in his relatively short life. I'm not a pilot or technical expert — it's the human dimension of these trailblazers' lives that interests me.

Once again the book was launched at Avid Reader Bookshop, Brisbane. As both a writer and reader I'm thankful that bookshops continue to survive in Australia's cultural landscape, especially the independent ones like Avid and Riverbend (both of which stock my books). I'm also grateful (and pleasantly surprised) to find my books in libraries across Australia (although I'm careful never to check to see how often they're borrowed.)

My modest success as a writer and my teaching experience has led to my becoming an invited mentor with the Queensland Writers Centre. This is a very satisfying role because it not only gives me an opportunity to encourage aspiring writers but has also introduced me to the wide range of topics those writers are passionate about. And, of course, as educators know, while I'm teaching I'm also learning.

University of NSW brain researcher Professor Perminder Sachdev says surviving into older age relies partly on 'a lifetime of good effort'. Some of that effort is a solid education in our formative years and then ongoing 'purposeful learning'. That purposeful learning can happen just as readily in a sewing circle, a bush care group, a men's shed and amongst family, friends and fellow workers, as in a structured 'educational' class with a teacher.

I'm thankful to my parents and school teachers for my own solid education base (although I suspect that at times both parties wondered if that was a lost cause).

That foundation has enhanced a lifetime of learning for me. It has given me not only a love of words, but also the urge to try to put them together as clearly and creatively as I can, for whatever audience I'm writing for at the time.

Queenslander – Alan Smith

James Vernon

SCHOOL AND OTHER DISTRACTIONS — A FIFTIES CHILDHOOD

The 1950s have a reputation for being rather boring. Yes, they were boring in the big picture. But the micro-view had a few good things going for it, especially for kids.

There was a general feeling of safety. Naturally, we were inculcated with the knowledge that we shouldn't speak to strangers and must never, never, never accept anything from a stranger. But strangers who might seduce us with such encouragement seemed to be almost mythical beings. Parents could acquire a few hours of privacy on a Saturday afternoon by dispatching the kids to the matinee at the local movie theatre. (Sixpence admission and sixpence for an ice cream.) How many kids returned home not realising they would soon have a sibling?

Houses were frequently left unattended and unlocked. Our home at Chelmer had a large, old-fashioned lock on the front door with a large, old-fashioned key that was never used. In fact, I think Dad took a couple of years to even realise that it had been broken and was jamming the lock. (I must admit to being the guilty party.) Well, there was no point locking the front door because there was no lock at all on the back door.

That was a good arrangement. If unexpected rain arrived after a woman had hung the washing on the line and then gone out, a neighbour would almost certainly notice the dry clothes, retrieve them from the line and enter through the unlocked door to deposit them on the kitchen table to await the owner's return.

The wheelie bin hadn't been invented in the 1950s and much of Brisbane didn't have access to a sewerage system despite numerous promises over several years to complete this important service. These facilities were provided by a contractor called Hunter Brothers.

The garbage bin was located at the back of the house. A truck would arrive once a week and a man with an empty bin on his shoulder would run down the side of the house and return at speed bearing the full bin that was then deposited in the truck.

Toilets were located in a little outhouse usually referred to as 'the dunny'. There was a large wooden box with a hole in it as a seat. A door in the box opened to reveal a large can. A box of sawdust with a scoop sat beside the seat. Sawdust was sprinkled in the can after it received its deposit, to absorb offensive odours. Generally speaking the arrangement was quite practical but wet weather caused a problem. This was partially solved by the use of a chamber pot, sometimes referred to as a 'gazunder'. (It GOES UNDER the bed). This would save the children from an unscheduled shower when it rained.

Loading a Hunter Brothers night soil truck 1963[1]

The can from the toilet was collected in a similar manner to the garbage bin. A truck stopped outside the house. A man jumped out and ran to the toilet and exchanged an empty can for the full one. This was perched precariously on his shoulder while he ran back to the truck. It isn't easy to run with a can of slops on your shoulder. I eventually realised that the need for speed was probably caused by an employer who set a very demanding schedule. Laundering the collector's work clothes must have been a very unpleasant task.

The householder's gratitude for their diligence was demonstrated every Christmas and Easter. A bottle of beer would be left on the toilet seat and the garbage bin as a sign of appreciation. The collectors would leave a card with a humorous poem about the service they provided.

---

1 www.facebook.com/Lost.Brisbane/photos/hunter-brothers-night-soil-treatment-facility-windsor-1963-photo-brisbane-city-c/862887403822362

Education of course was a product of the society it served. In my case primary education was delivered with varying quality by the Presentation nuns at the Graceville convent.

I remember my first day there. For some time I had been indoctrinated with the idea of 'going to school'. Older siblings disappeared in the morning and reappeared magically in the afternoon, having spent their day 'at school'. The first day passed happily enough but I couldn't really understand why it was necessary to return the next day. After all, I had 'been to school', hadn't I? That feeling persisted for the next twelve years.

To be honest, primary school wasn't too bad although a bit strange at times. While I have to admit that some of the nuns had some rather peculiar beliefs and practices, I didn't observe any of the brutality for which some have become infamous.

There were exceptions of course:

> *Sister Ita is a biter,*
> *She goes to Mass on Sunday*
> *to ask God for the strength*
> *to WHACK the kids on Monday.*

But, to be fair, even she wasn't all that bad.

The worst crime the education system committed on childhood was probably hypocrisy.

Schools played their part in establishing gender and other stereotypes. As wide-eyed infants we sat on the floor and encouraged to recite:

What are little girls made of?
Sugar and spice and all things nice.
What are little boys made of?
Snakes and snails and puppy dogs' tails.

I declined the opportunity to participate in this sexist indoctrination and sat in sullen silence.

I also remember the day I became a racist. I was sitting on the floor carrying out some mindless task deemed suitable for grade 2. Mother Carmel (from Ireland) was circulating, supervising and big-noting herself to the couple of mothers who were assisting. 'I don't know why Australians make so much of being a "real" Australian,' she said. 'To be a "real" Australian you have to be descended from either a convict or an Aborigine.'

In her telling, both antecedents seemed equally undesirable. The problem with convict descent was obvious. Possessing Aboriginal ancestors must have carried a similar stain.

But on reflection and to be fair, she was probably as much a victim of society as her charges were. The official government position was that people of different skin colours couldn't live together peacefully. Conflict would be inevitable. This official position was perpetuated through the curriculum and was generally accepted as a universal truth. This makes education sound like indoctrination. Very largely it was.

I also remember when I ceased being a racist, and equally importantly, started to question the wisdom and truthfulness of the powers that be. This is a characteristic that is still with me. Winifred Atwell was a very popular Jamaican 'honky tonk' pianist in the 50s and I was one of her fans. When I was in grade 6 I was delighted to read that she had enjoyed her extensive Australian tour so much that she wanted to migrate here permanently. A few days later I was dismayed to read that she was not acceptable as an immigrant because she was black. Well, she was of Jamaican descent.

No matter how much I thought about this I couldn't see how a middle-aged, matronly musician could be a threat to the welfare and social fabric of Australia. Obviously we were being taught lies in school. Web research has revealed that she was eventually accepted on our hallowed shores in the early 70s and received citizenship due to her character and talent a couple of years before her death. (I should point out that although I found references to her tour in the 50s, I didn't find any reference to her earlier refused attempt to migrate here. However, there are inconsistencies in the information on the web.)

As we grew there were unwritten expectations that were somehow regarded as being obvious and natural. Little girls were encouraged to learn the piano or violin from one of the nuns. The few boys who were subjected to this indignity seemed to be 'different' in the eyes of their peers and usually had a short musical career. If piano were suspect, the violin had a definite proscription on the grounds of being not quite masculine.

Of course, every child needed to be able to speak 'nicely' and elocution lessons were highly regarded by some.

The girls (usually the ones who were given piano lessons) had one set of texts: 'Uncle John, have you seen my mouse? He must be somewhere about the house.' The boys, (the ones who couldn't lie, feign illness or run fast enough), had their own: 'If only I had some money! I'd buy a jolly boat.'

These literary masterpieces were delivered with beautifully rounded vowels of the 'How now, brown cow' variety. Well, they practised this nonsense assiduously to the approbation of Sister What'shername and their parents, then left the room and used their authentic working class vernacular as soon as they were through the door.

Immigration at the time was a key factor in Australian society. Until World War II our importation of people had been mainly satisfied by immigration from the 'Mother Country'. After the war many British were needed for rebuilding their own homeland.

This led Australia to accept what many regarded as less desirable immigrants from central, eastern and southern Europe. Their offspring were represented at school, of course. My surroundings had quite a large Polish population.

It was one of these Poles that gave me a slight inkling of why they had left their own country. My family had been invited to a Sunday afternoon tea by the mother of one of my classmates. At one point in the conversation she described the sight of the sky being 'black with 'planes' and the fear it induced as well as seeing part of her city 'smashed to pieces'. It was very easy to sense the feelings behind the words.

Other cultural differences also appeared. On one occasion one of the nuns became suspicious of the group of us around a German kid as we were decorating the back of our hands with a pen. Her investigation was followed by an outburst that left Christ's dealing with the moneychangers at the temple looking as if He were simply dissatisfied with the rate of exchange He was being offered! I'm sure her tirade would have had much greater impact if she had thought to explain the significance of the swastika.

The swastika got the same kid in trouble a couple of weeks later. He removed the blade from his pencil sharpener and cut the accursed symbol into the palms of both himself and an Australian boy. I think he left the school shortly after.

When I was doing my education pre-service training I was given an assignment to write about the teacher I admired most. This was a problem as admirable teachers in my life were rare. Then I remembered Sister Elizabeth, my only truly admirable teacher. She possessed all of the professional and personal attributes that we were being encouraged to emulate. She praised creativity and had a genuine concern for the well-being of her charges that wasn't restricted to their Immortal Souls.

True, we still had a lot of rote learning. Having mastered the twelve times table we were encouraged to extend ourselves up to the twenty-five times table. I have to admit that, although tedious, this was rather useful in later years in negotiating day-to-day arithmetic tasks.

Having memorised 'Mark Antony's oration' (boys), and 'The quality of mercy is not strained' (girls) from the reading book, we were encouraged to perform them for the class. That is, if competing for the loudest declamation can be regarded as performance. But it was fun and I still enjoy Shakespeare.

Of course, life went on outside of home and school. There were the local playgrounds. The first and best of these was the local dump, also referred to as 'The Swamp'. It was an expanse of smelly green ooze that the council was using as land fill to create the football field near Chelmer Railway Station. Provided we could avoid the dump trucks, irate council workers and the green slime, it was a veritable treasure trove of useless stuff of temporary desirability. Naturally, it was a strict no-go zone. There was one memorable occasion when I paid a surreptitious visit only to place a clumsy foot into a large, deep puddle of green muck. Normally I could have talked my way around it but the state of that sand shoe was completely inexplicable.

However, the dump did produce some good stuff, namely two dilapidated bikes and a scooter. All three articles were lovingly restored. The latter, fixed up in secrecy, became my birthday present from my siblings. They also used their restored bikes in a futile attempt to overcome my atrocious balance and teach me to ride. Loss of skin caused Dad to forbid this activity in the interest of my safety. (I don't think this prohibition caused them any grief. Well, I was also endangering their bikes.) Wheels! Wow!

The other was more conventional — the cricket field at Graceville Park. This provided a number of diversions. At times the boys were allowed to go there at lunchtime to play football, totally unsupervised. Well, that might not be completely true. Although there were no teachers, nuns, priests or other nuisances to supervise us, there was the 50s version of Neighbourhood Watch as we learned. On one occasion the game got a bit too rough. Suddenly a virago appeared on the field and gave us a tongue-lashing that even the angriest teacher would have been proud of.

Then she disappeared back to her own territory after admonishing us that if we didn't 'play nicely' she'd ring the convent.

The park provided a number of distractions apart from that. There was the old draught horse that was used to pull the mower and the huge roller for the pitch. We had many warnings that he had a bad temper and we should stay well clear of him. That was just an adult scare tactic. I don't know of his ever acting cantankerously. He would just munch away while looking at us with a superior attitude and snort loudly if we impinged on his territory. Still, he was awfully big. Prudence was advisable.

Naturally, there was the obligatory playground with its swings, climbing tower, hanging bars, turntable and other sites for awful accidents. When I got tired of those instruments of torture there was the mound of pitch that was used to repair the cricket wicket.

This really had limited attraction apart from the fact that it was excavated into a concave shape that provided some measure of concealment for an illicit cigarette. The pitch itself was reasonable modelling clay but I didn't produce anything that warranted preservation so theft of pitch never featured in the confessional.

They were the boring activities in the park for most of the boring year. However, every year the big event arrived without any fanfare — either Ashton's, Wirth's or Bullen Bros' CIRCUS!

On the way to school the park would be the usual boring wasteland. By the time we trudged home a large part of it would be converted into a veritable wonderland. The Big Top tent. Cages with a variety of exotic animals. A rather bored-looking elephant tethered by a thick chain. And activity. Foul-mouthed, impatient men swinging large hammers, tying ropes and making very precise suggestions about what the kids could do and where they could go to do it.

The appearance of a circus tent created great excitement when I was growing up [2]

It was very educational. Not only did we learn about the animals from the little cards on the cages but our linguistic ability was expanded by what we heard. An exchange between two workers:

'OwyagoinJack?'

'Lousy. Just scratching me arse with me toenail.'

What a pity such colourful expressions were proscribed for Good Kids.

---

2 www.ashtonentertainment.com.au/about-ashton-circus

Still, it was enough to inspire a spontaneous outburst of song. Well, the outburst usually had to be confined to mental melody in case an adult or, even worse, a parent, should hear:

> *Ask your mother for sixpence to see the big giraffe,*
> *With pimples on its eyebrows*
> *And pimples on its ——*
> *Ask your mother for sixpence to buy a bottle of sarse,*
> *And go and find a policeman*
> *And ram it up his ——*
> *Ask your mother for sixpence...*

Etc., etc., etc., ad infinitum.

Unfortunately, sixpence wouldn't cover admission to the circus, so seeing the performance was rare. Only once.

Then came a huge change which had a marked influence in my formative years. We took over the boarding house when I was in year 7 — aged 12, I think. It was a big change. We went from a small house on the flats at Chelmer to a huge house on a quite steep hill at Taringa. (If I remember correctly it had seven bedrooms and two 'sleepouts'.)

Instead of living as a nuclear family we shared the place with up to eight other people. I not only had my own room, one of the 'sleepouts', but I had to travel by train to school every day. These two aspects gave me plenty of time alone. The latter gave me the opportunity to supplement my income as a 'stringer' (collecting sports results for the Saturday evening edition of the *Telegraph* newspaper), by travelling without a ticket to school.

That job gave me the opportunity to observe another aspect of Australian society. At the time, soccer was played mainly by European immigrants. True football fans often claimed it was played by weaklings because of the lack of officially sanctioned body contact, and they stayed with rugby and Australian rules. Many of the soccer teams consisted of cultural groups.

Australians tended to think in national groups such as Jugoslavs, Italians and Greeks without realising that these nationalities were formed by different ethnic groups. It was these individual groups that came together to form teams. The problem was that some of these formations had major historic grievances that were played out on the field in some quite serious episodes of violence.

Although the fifties might have had a lot of boring predictability, they provided an important historical pivot point. The ideological basis for the wars of the earlier twentieth century was replaced by the ideological foundation for the different type of warfare practised in the second half of the century.

I'm very pleased that my early questioning of authority continued into adulthood.

Offcuts 2

St John's Oxley – Peter Darmody

Dave Shearer

LIGHTHOUSE SERVICE

Now it's not every day you glance up and read a sign mounted above a doorway and think to yourself, 'That looks interesting!'

Well, back in 1972 I was walking up the main street of Port Adelaide in South Australia, next to the old historic building and there was a sign above the old historic building entrance door which read 'Commonwealth Lighthouse Service.' For a few seconds I wondered what it was all about. However, there was shopping to be done so the thought vanished from my mind as I continued walking up the street.

A few months later while I was working as a maintenance fitter at the Mail Exchange with Australia Post in Adelaide City I had the opportunity to read the *Federal Government Monthly Gazette* which advertised employment positions right around Australia. This was the one that was published early in the year, which advertised positions available within the Federal Government. So, as I was running my finger down the list I came across Lighthouse Service positions. It brought back the memory of the Port Adelaide Office.

So, a few days later I investigated it further. I ended up back at the office door at the Port. I walked in and knocked on the door of the first office. Unbeknown to me it was the CEO's office. I explained why I was there and he was quite polite and gave me a quick rundown of the position, but suggested I visit the depot workshop which was only 200 metres back down the street. He proposed I talk to the workshop supervisor, Paul Savage.

So I fronted up down there and Paul gave me a tour of the depot. The workshop was only small but well equipped. While talking to Paul I explained my military background as an Army apprentice. He informed me that he had done his apprenticeship in a local Army workshop as a civilian. I had never heard of that happening before, so we definitely had something in common. At the end of the tour I asked Paul, 'How often does this type of job come up?' He replied, 'Not very often,' but to keep an eye on the Saturday's employment section in the local paper.

When I got back home I said to my wife Maree, 'I can forget about the job on the lighthouses. It only comes up every 15 to 20 years.'

Nevertheless, I kept an eye out in the Saturday paper as I was looking for another job along the way. A fortnight later there it was! A position with the Federal Government for a lighthouse mechanic. I couldn't believe my eyes!

Unbeknown to me one of the lighthouse mechanics had had an accident at one of the manned stations in the engine room. He'd injured his right eye a month or two before, and unfortunately had been medically discharged from the department with impaired vision. I quickly wrote up my qualifications and submitted them for the position. A week later I received a letter to attend an interview at the Port Adelaide office.

Original chest pocket off my work overalls

The interview was very official — three clerical staff and Paul Savage on one side of a long desk and me on the other side sitting on a single chair — being cross-examined by all of them. Finally, Paul asked if I could go down to the depot again for a trade test examination and speak to Murray Foote.

I arrived down at the depot and told Murray what I was there for. He said, 'What do they want you to do?'

I replied, 'I don't know. You will have to tell me!'

So, he walked over and picked up a piece of steel bar and a one-inch Whitworth nut. He came back and said, 'Cut me a thread to suit this nut.'

I took a big gulp as I had not operated a lathe for about seven years. Having been posted to aviation within the army, it was a no-no to manufacture any kind of aircraft parts. Anyway, I set up the lathe to the best of my memory, ground the tool bit up to suit the thread and away I went. Three-quarters of an hour later I spun the steel piece on the nut. And that was it.

I took it back to Murray and he said, 'Very good', and then threw it in the bin!

So home I went and waited with fingers crossed for another week, hoping for a reply from the Department. All went in my favour and I was successful in getting the appointment. Later I was told there were numerous applicants for the position, but I will admit I think my previous visit to the depot had sealed the deal.

This started my career adventure with the Lighthouse Service for over the next twenty years.

ALWAYS CHECK THE MENU!

Now you don't tell everybody that you took up backpacking when you retired, because that should have been done when you were 19 years of age — or even 25 if you were a late starter! However, my wife Maree and I, who have camped around Australia for many years, thought the idea sounded very exciting. So, this is just one story of our many adventures across South-east Asia after I retired.

We travelled by train from Hanoi City in Vietnam directly north to the Chinese border. I remember it well because even before the train departed the main station, the conductor was walking along the platform checking the train. When he came to our carriage he tapped on the window and pointed at my backpack which I had placed on the parcel rack above our heads. I was a little confused to start with as I had placed it in what I though was a safe position. He continued pointing up at the pack and then down to the floor. I could see by the expression on his face that he was not happy. The carriage was some years old but solidly built with steel brackets supporting the rack and very well screwed into the carriage wall. But when you are a visitor in a strange country you must abide by the rules. I lifted my pack down on the floor and he gave me a stern look and then a nod and continued on up the railway platform. I smiled to myself and thought, 'Welcome to Vietnam Rail!'

We left the train at the border and caught a small forty-year-old bus westward into the mountains on a windy dirt road filled with potholes. We hoped the driver had done the trip before and the brakes on the bus were okay. The scenery was breathtaking and we passed many 'hill people' walking many kilometres into the nearest town, carrying food and supplies on their heads and backs.

Finally, we arrived at the hill town of Sapa, built on the side of the mountain with a steep main street. It had many small shops, eateries, markets and accommodation. The next two days we wandered around and explored the town. We hired an old Russian motorbike and ventured out of town for fifteen to twenty kilometres on a rough hill road for more of a look about.

The local mountain people were dressed in their traditional clothing, which was very colourful, adorned with their home-made jewellery. One older woman came up and stood quite close to me and pulled out an old matchbox and looked up at me and said, 'Do you want to buy?' I was a bit curious and asked her, 'What is it?' She then pushed the box open and the contents looked like dried flowers, but I said, 'No, not today, but thanks!' When I told Maree, she laughed and said, 'Get with it, that was mountain-grown marijuana!' So, I had just knocked back a top-shelf deal for the day!

The next morning our guesthouse informed us we had to move out as the place was 'full' — this is the Asian term for 'This accommodation is booked out with other guests.' So we grabbed our backpacks and wandered around town looking for somewhere else to stay. This proved difficult as the next day was 'May Day' and the locals were all in town to celebrate. After two hours of searching we thought the local park bench was starting to look good! Finally, we ended up down the bottom end of the main street in a two-storey local restaurant with an offer of accommodation on the roof. We said, 'On the roof?!', but upon inspection it was just one room, clean and tidy with two beds and complete with a light.

When we went back down to pay our $5.00 overnight fee the fellow behind the desk said, 'You no eat here,' but I said to him we were happy to eat Vietnamese food. But he said again, 'You NO eat here, you go up the street to where the tourists eat!' Okay, no more arguing. So we went off and had a tasty meal with a cold local beer.

On our return we had to walk through the main café, which was feeding thirty to forty locals, then out the back past the kitchen and up the stairs onto the roof area. When we walked over to the handrails on the side of the building and looked out at the million dollar view back down the mountain and across the valley and country side, we were impressed. Five American dollars had been well spent.

We slept well through the night. However, I woke up early to the sound of a dog whimpering. About twenty minutes later I heard a big crunching sound and the dog stopped whimpering. I then went back to sleep. Later we got up and dressed for breakfast, passing back down through the ground floor with many locals enjoying breakfast, eating out of their bowls with plenty of rice and fried meat, using their traditional chop-sticks. So up the street we went again for our breakfast.

After ordering I casually said to Maree, 'Did you hear the dog whimpering this morning?'

Without looking up she answered, 'I don't want to talk about the poor dog.'

So, with an answer like that, it confirmed my own thoughts on what might have been on the breakfast menu for the locals back at our accommodation.

Matchbox – Dave Shearer

Lighthouse – Brian Goeldner

George Pugh

MAJOR CRIMES

Some major crimes are not solved, but some are solved by good luck or good detective work!

Major Shooting Incident

On 12 March 1984, I was a Detective at the Woolloongabba Criminal Investigation Branch, working the 6 am to 2 pm shift.

During this shift I was tasked to investigate a shooting at the Painters and Dockers' shed, Kangaroo Point, which was situated under the Story Bridge at the Woolloongabba end.

On arrival at the Painters and Dockers' shed, I went inside and observed a large pool of blood on the floor, which was being mopped up by a member of the Painter and Dockers. I ordered this person to stop mopping up the blood and asked him what had happened. I was informed that, when another member of the Painter and Dockers went to take the rubbish out to the bin, he was shot in his left shoulder and arm.

I arranged for police to guard the scene of the shooting and ordered a scientific examination, after which I went to the Royal

Brisbane Hospital to interview the wounded man who also turned out to be a union official.

When interviewed the man would only tell me his name and address. He refused to tell me the circumstances of his shooting. In fact, the victim would not even admit that he had suffered an injury to his left arm caused by a gun fired at short range.

I believed that, going on the blood on the floor of the Painters and Dockers' shed which trailed in from the outside, the victim had been shot near the rubbish bin and had run back inside the building.

I managed to obtain information from one of the painters and dockers at the shed that the victim was shot for cheating on the overtime. He said the victim would put the names of everyone wanting to work overtime on a piece of paper into a hat, and the name on the sheet that was drawn out would be the one to work the overtime. However, the victim's name was consistently drawn out of the hat to work overtime, so another member of the painter and dockers checked the names in the hat. It was then found that all the pieces of paper in the hat had the victim's name on them. No other members' names were in the hat.

In company with another detective, I conducted inquiries about the shooting. We interviewed members of the Brisbane Painter and Dockers, in an attempt to identify the person or persons responsible.

During my investigation, I received information from a member of the public, who wished to remain anonymous, that he had hooked a sawn-off .22 rifle that had been modified for a silencer whilst fishing in the Brisbane River near the Colmslie Boat Ramp. This was about 8 km from the shooting scene at Kangaroo Point.

I arranged to meet the informant and took possession of the modified firearm.

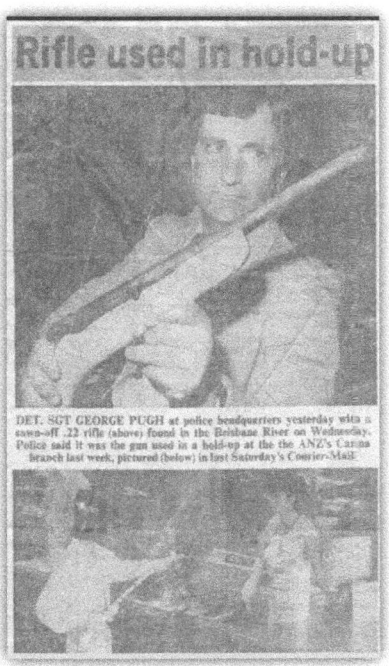

A further anonymous phone caller informed me that he had allegedly seen the victim of the shooting being dragged into a blue Ford Fairlane sedan bearing Queensland number plates at about 7 am on the day of the shooting, but the victim struggled with the two men and managed to escape.

The other detective and I, although working hard on the investigation and believing that the shooter was a member of the Brisbane Painters and Dockers, were unable to identify the offender.

One day I received a call from the president of the Painters and Dockers, Brisbane, who requested that I meet with him at 4 pm in the private bar of the Balmoral Hotel, Balmoral, which was the drinking hole of all the painters and dockers in that area.

On arriving at the Balmoral Hotel I knew that I was taking a big risk so I decided that I and the other detective would lock our handguns (.38 snub nose revolvers) in the glovebox of our police vehicle, so that no one could disarm us and use our weapons on us.

On entering the private bar I observed that there were five painters and dockers in the private bar. Two of them were playing pool near the entrance to the bar and there were two other men seated at a table at the other end.

The painter and docker who was standing in the middle of the bar, motioned me and my partner to join him.

The painter and docker introduced himself to us as the president of the Painters and Dockers of Brisbane, and then commenced to abuse us for harassing his members over the shooting of the painter and docker at their office at Kangaroo Point. During this standoff, which lasted for about 10 minutes, the President told me to 'drop off' investigating the shooting, stating that we were both wasting our time as his members would not talk to us anyway. The President went on to inform us that it would look good for him in the eyes of his members if the investigating officers would agree to stop our investigation of this shooting.

After a discussion with my partner, I told the President that as our investigation was not getting anywhere near solving the shooting, I would agree to drop off and stop the investigation. The President was pleased with the agreement to end the police investigation.

The shooting of the painter and docker at Kangaroo Point has remained unsolved to this day.

BAD LUCK BANK ROBBERIES

Armed Robbery of Commonwealth Bank, Newstead

A bank robber entered the Commonwealth Bank, Newstead, armed with a long barrelled rifle. Waving the rifle in a threatening manner, he ordered everyone inside the bank to 'GET ON THE FLOOR.'

Everyone inside the bank, including a recently retired detective, obeyed the bank robber's instructions and got on the floor.

The detective had recently retired from the Queensland Police Force as he and his wife had decided to set up a business selling mobile phones, which had just started to enter the market. He was at the bank to deposit his weekly takings.

The retired detective later informed the investigating police that as he was no longer in the police force, he was one of the first bank customers to 'hit the floor'. He had no intention of trying to stop the robbery.

The retired detective informed the police that he could hear the bank robber yelling and on looking up from where he was lying on the floor, he saw the robber hitting an 'old digger' with the rifle and ordering him to the ground. The old digger, who was aged about 85 years, was standing at the counter of the bank leaning on a walking cane and refusing to get on the floor.

The retired detective informed the police that on seeing the bank robber attacking the old digger, he suddenly jumped up and tackled the robber to the floor.

In the struggle, the rifle discharged, killing the bank robber.

Armed Robbery of Chardon's Corner Hotel Bottle Shop, Annerley

Two men decided to rob the Chardon's Corner Hotel bottle shop at Annerley, and planned it to perfection. They bought handguns and face masks and stole a motor vehicle to use as a 'getaway car'. The two also agreed they'd take only paper banknotes as bagged coins were too heavy to carry whilst running from the robbery.

On the day of the robbery, they left the stolen 'getaway car' in a side street about 600 metres from the bottle shop. They then put on their masks and, armed with their handguns, entered the bottle shop of the hotel and ordered the staff to put all the paper cash into the bags they were carrying.

The robbery went as planned. The staff filled their bags with cash and the robbers then ran out of the bottle shop towards the side street where they had left their stolen 'getaway car'.

However, on arrival they discovered that someone had stolen their stolen getaway vehicle!

The two robbers were now in a panic as they could hear police sirens. They ran to a taxi rank and caught a taxi home.

Unknown to the two bank robbers was that one of the first police procedures when investigating a bank robbery is that Police Communications contact the Taxi Communications operative to inquire if any taxi has picked up anyone near the robbery. In this case, the Police Communications Centre was advised that a taxi had picked up two suspicious male persons near the Chardon's

Corner Hotel and had taken them to an address at Moorooka.

The police went to the address at Moorooka and found the two robbers inside counting the stolen money from the bottle shop, and arrested them.

Armed Robbery of Westpac Bank, Stones Corner

A lone male bank robber entered the Westpac Bank at Stones Corner armed with a handgun, and ordered several customers not to move. He pointed the handgun at a female bank teller, ordering her to fill up a bag that he gave her with *'BANK NOTES ONLY'*.

The female bank teller did as she was told and on being handed the bag the bank robber ran from the bank and made his getaway in a stolen motor vehicle.

However, one of the bank customers, who was in possession of a Panasonic mobile phone, one of the first mobile phones on the market at that time, ran to his motor vehicle parked outside the bank and gave chase.

As the bank customer followed the bank robber, who was speeding away in his stolen motor vehicle along Logan Road towards Mount Gravatt, he used his mobile phone and reported the armed robbery to the Queensland Police Communications Centre, informing the police that he was following the robber in his own motor vehicle. On receiving the information the police were mobilised and joined in the chase.

Offcuts 2

Police car – George Pugh

As the bank customer followed the bank robber along Logan Road towards Mount Gravatt, he reported that the bank robber had disappeared under a block of units. Waiting outside on the roadway, the bank customer saw the robber emerge from the block of units. However, he had changed his clothes and was now using a pushbike in his getaway attempt.

Using his mobile phone, the bank customer reported this new development to the Police Communications Centre, and the bank robber was immediately apprehended by police.

If it hadn't been for the invention of the Panasonic mobile phone (called 'The Brick' because it included a very heavy two-kilo battery), the robber, by changing his clothes, ditching his stolen getaway motor vehicle, and riding away on a push bike, would have pulled off the perfect bank robbery.

ATTACK ON YOUNG WOMAN, STONES CORNER, BRISBANE

Background

In April 1976 a young schoolteacher went to a photographic studio in Stones Corner, Brisbane, to have her 21st birthday portrait taken. On returning to her parked motor vehicle she was abducted by a male person armed with a knife and viciously raped in a nearby park.

Immediately following the rape the offender tried to kill the woman by trying to strangle her with the leg of her jeans. Although terrified, but desperate to try to stop the offender from killing her, the woman used 'reverse psychology', telling the offender that she loved him. She promised that she would not report the rape to the police.

The offender believed the woman, allowing her to go free. On returning home, she immediately reported the rape to the police.

The Investigation

Another detective and I were assigned to investigate the alleged rape. We interviewed the rape victim, who described the offender to us. She informed us that the offender had a tattoo in the shape of a heart with the word 'KAREN' on his right arm, and that he had short hair.

From that description, I knew that there were two possibilities — either the offender was recently released from prison or was a member of the Australian Defence Force.

Offcuts 2

As I knew that the Records Section of Boggo Road Jail, Annerley, kept records of prisoners, I went there and spoke to staff. I told them that the offender had a tattoo in the form of a heart with the word 'KAREN' on his right arm. To my surprise the staff member informed me that he had seen a recently released prisoner's file on his desk with such a tattoo and showed me the file.

I wrote down the details of the prisoner's record, name, address, tattoos etc., then went back to the office and put together a photographic board of 12 photographs of similar looking criminals on the police data base. Of course, the board included the photo of the recently released prisoner from Boggo Road Jail.

On viewing the photographic board, the rape victim immediately identified the rapist and collapsed in shock.

Armed with this evidence, I and five other detectives raided the offender's house at Annerley at 6 am the next day. On entering his home we were confronted by the offender's wife, who told us that her husband did not live there anymore. Our search of the house failed to locate him.

On driving away from the premises I stopped the police vehicle and said to my partner, 'Did you see the pair of men's hiking boots in the lounge?' and he said, 'Yes.' So I turned the police vehicle around and went back.

On arrival I walked to the back of the offender's house. I noticed a man walking down the back stairs of the house next door, drinking a stubbie of beer. I called out to him, telling him I was a detective and asked him who lived in the house. He said, 'I don't know,' and kept on walking.

I immediately became suspicious and walked up the back stairs of the house, which was an old Queensland-style home — kitchen in the back, and bedrooms off the central hallway which led to the front veranda and front door.

I had my police revolver in my right hand and quickly searched each bedroom. On reaching the front veranda I noticed something strange. There was a single metal bed without a mattress, and a pile of washing on the floor with the mattress on top of the clothes.

On lifting up the mattress I found the offender hiding underneath. I quickly arrested him, placing him in handcuffs. (On hearing me entering the house, he had raced to the front verandah, jumped on the pile of clothing on the bed and pulled the mattress off the bed, hiding underneath with the pile of clothes.)

I subsequently charged the offender with rape and attempted murder of the young schoolteacher, and he was remanded in custody.

Detective Inspector George Pugh

Offcuts 2

Committal Hearing and Trial

At the committal hearing of the charges in the Brisbane Magistrates Court some months later, I was approached by the rape victim's father, a tough hard-working cane farmer from Bowen in north Queensland. He said to me, 'What would happen to me if I jumped over there...' — pointing to the 'dock' where the offender was sitting, '... and strangled that shit-house?'

I said, 'No, I can't let you do that.' (If I had known then how he had destroyed the lives of the victim and her family, I would have said, 'Wait till I leave the court room.')

He replied, 'But that's *what I want to do*. He has destroyed my family. We are all sad and my daughter has changed from a nice loving daughter into something else. She was engaged to be married when she was raped.'

I had noticed a change in his daughter myself, and following telephone calls to me from her distraught family in Bowen, I invited her and her fiancé to my home for a family barbeque, just to assure her that I did respect her. However, she never married.

The offender was committed for trial to the Supreme Court, Brisbane, three months later, where he pleaded 'Guilty' to all charges and was sentenced to a term of imprisonment of seven years.

Birds – Anthony Durrington

John Brown

THE SMELL OF NEW-MOWN HAY

Scythe and sickle use heralded my initiation into the field of agricultural pursuits.

Dad was nipping a patch of Scotch thistle in the bud, to prevent them forming their beautiful pink flower heads and maturing seed that would be blown in the wind. I had seen the increasing patches of the robust pest take hold in the grass paddocks and had watched him hone his blade before cutting them down at ground level. I was using the sickle when he said, 'Here boy, have a go,' and handed me the scythe.

My apprenticeship as a hay maker began in Victoria in 1942 in an oats paddock along the left side of the Coleraine-Casterton Road at the foot of the steep Muntham Hill.

First World War returning soldiers had been allocated small acreage farms in the Coleraine district and they and their families eked out a living with small-scale dairying and the growing grain crops such as oats, barley, wheat and corn. Nearly every farmer had dairy cows, sending their cream to the Coleraine Butter Factory and using the skim milk to feed their pigs. Fodder needed to be grown to feed the working horses and to supplement feed other livestock, in the dry summer months.

It was late December 1941 and the crops were ripening each day. The young men were all away fighting the dreadful Second World War and the older men were called on to keep the home fires burning by ensuring life carried on until they returned.

The day dawned hot and the sun appeared, sending its red ball over the distant Grampians and flooding its light across the hills and fertile flats where the silted creek delta widened and formed. The water from the creek was fed by its tributaries, taking the water from the surrounding valleys. It flowed at a right angle into the Wannon and then onto the Glenelg River, the water eventually finding its way by zig-zag course into the sea near Nelson.

Oat crops that year had benefited by a wetter than usual spring rainfall and had long stalks and robust heads full of grain. There was a light morning breeze coming down the valley, sending a ripple like the waves of a calm sea. I was just thirteen and Dad had kept me home from school to help him and three other men. His task was to make stooks of the binder-harvested oaten hay on the property on the Casterton Road.

The author, aged 13

As the day warmed up, a summer north wind with a burning sun beating down heralded an uncomfortable day ahead for us. There was a short wait and a chat among the men as the contractor with his horse-drawn harvester binder set-up surveyed the crop to decide the best way to start. It was an operation far different from the way we harvest agricultural crops today.

Stooking of hay meant standing up to a dozen or more sheaves on their cut ends and slanting with the seed tops to the centre, resembling teepees and making the finished paddock look like an Indian camp.

Etched in my memory all these years later is the smell of new-mown hay as the cutting blade was lowered to stubble height and the driver took a full circle into the edge of the crop to ensure all was ready to go. Then, with his two well-trained draught horses obeying his commands he began runs around the field for the six hours it took to complete the sheaf-making, experiencing only two hold-ups to replace broken cutter blades. It gave us time to catch up but in the end we were left with two more hours to finish our Indian camp. After the last sheaf was tossed out, the tired and sweating horses were unharnessed, fed and watered and given a good rub down by a proud horse owner.

The stalks were cut at about six inches above ground and dropped onto a conveyer belt that took them to the binder twine-tying apparatus, which could be pre-adjusted to give the size of the sheaves required according to the maturity of the crop. Once the sheaves were tied they were conveyed to the slide chute and spilled cut-end to the ground.

We finished our task at about four o'clock, just as the farmer's wife and his two pretty daughters arrived with refreshments. The pretty daughters took my eye and put a spark in my thoughts. Eight years later that spark for one of them kindled a burning flame that led me to a marriage that gave a life of love, joy and bliss, and to me becoming the patriarch of a family of three children, seven grandchildren, and ten great grandchildren.

They had brought cold tea and a few bottles of cold beer. I took my eyes off the girls for a few moments and watched as their mother poured each of the men a full chipped enamel cup of beer.

Dad looked at me and then the lady before saying, 'What about one for the boy? He has done a hard day's work.' That was my first beer and I have yet to taste a better one.

The sun was sinking behind the hill as we were leaving. A puff of dust heralded the start of a whirlwind that took a meandering course through the stubble, taking with it dust and loose straw but not the pleasant memories of my first harvest day.

Oat grain and hay made excellent fodder for livestock. For harvesting, timing for storage was necessary to ensure the hay was dry enough to prevent heating when stacked but not too dried out to shed its grain. I was also involved with this harvest with the collecting, stack-making and chaff-cutting.

Oats that were planted in late winter or in early spring seeded in December and were ready for harvester heading around Christmas time, but harvesting for hay was binder-harvested early, with the sap still in the stalks and with the seeds retaining their nutrient. This crop was harvested for use on the farm.

The hay was collected by horse-drawn wagon with a person on the wagon expertly arranging the sheaves to ensure the shiny smooth stalks were bound in such a way that no ropes were needed to tie down the load for transport to the haystack site. Pronged pitchforks, lightweight and long-handled for pitching high, were the implements used for gathering the sheaves and also for the other hay operation tasks.

Haystack-making required careful binding of the layers by placing of the sheaves so as to provide a waterproof overhang tent-like roof top. Many stacks stood in the paddocks with the quality of the hay unimpaired for years.

The ripened oat seed after cutting was separated from the sheaf heads in the threshing machine, leaving the stalks for chaff-making. Threshers and chaff cutters were driven by belts powered from a tractor or engine pulley.

A thresher was used to separate grain from the stalks, and the straw was used for chaff and made good stuffing for bed mattresses.

For better quality chaff more heads were left to go through the chaffcutter, but too much grain could cause problems in horses and other animals, such as impaction and colic. The crops that were cut at the right stage to keep their nutrients made excellent fodder for stock. Some of the crop was made into a haystack and the rest threshed, the grain bagged and stalks made into chaff.

I was involved in most of the operation in regard to this crop, and the experience was the beginning of my apprenticeship in the field of agriculture. Skills came only through toil and learning the hard way.

Another day, Dad kept me out of school to help. This time it was to thresh some of the crop and this was a new experience for me.

I had seen my parents with loose hay on a tarpaulin, using a stick to separate the seed from the stalks. I had been told of the way a person at the bottom of an elevator untied sheaves and teased the stalks to be carried to the person at the top, whose task it was to make sure that the heads were separated from the stalks.

I was surprised to find us at a shed with a threshing machine operated by a wide drive belt from a wheel mounted on a one-piston engine. The hay was brought by wagon from the haystack we had made a few days after that hot day which was drawn up alongside the thresher.

The machinery started and then we took it in turns removing the binder twine and pitching the hay into the hopper, then bagging the grain and getting the separated hay ready for making into chaff. The chaff bags were larger, lighter and more open than that of the grain bags.

HAY GROWING, AND HARVESTING

Three years later the scene had changed and I was working on a sheep property seventeen miles from Coleraine, the only one helping the farmer with running the property. It was my task to keep down the rabbits, tend the sheep and do the farm chores. The property was near Pigeon Ponds settlement on the plateau on the Horsham side of the Grampians and was mainly light loamy soil.

 Ploughing was not necessary when planting crops, including clover and ryegrass seed. Combines with cultivating feet and self-seeding and fertilising compartments had replaced the plough, allowing improvement of the pasture to be done in one operation. My boss had purchased a new tractor with power take-off and would drive the rig with me standing on a narrow wooden platform on the back of the combine ensuring that the fertiliser and the seed were flowing freely through the tubes connected to the cultivating feet.

Superphosphate would increase the carrying capacity of a paddock from one sheep to the acre to three or more. It was rationed during the war and, if used wisely to fertilise a paddock, could result in a high-quality hay harvest.

Shearing took place in late September. A twenty-acre holding paddock close to the shearing shed was used to hold sheep to be taken to the shed next day. Their constant droppings added to soil quality. We used superphosphate on this paddock as well, making the growth of the pasture even better.

I should now mention briefly the farm horse Bell, a light draught roan mare that could be ridden, used in a dray cart, hay rake, trace chains or any other farm work. She was truly the work horse on this farm.

The soft sandy soil in wet seasons would become like quicksand in places and your horse would sometimes bog to the belly. It was far worse if my horse Bell was pulling the spring cart.

Fortunately she seemed to realise that this was no time for impatience, and she would calmly wait until I could unharness her from the rig and allow her to flounder to more stable ground. With the straps buckled underneath her, freeing her from the harness and shafts was no easy task. When she was released there was still the problem of getting the cart out of the bog, and this often took an hour or more. I would tie a rope to the spoke of one wheel and use Bell to ease it out by first one wheel and then the other, until we were on sound footing again. That horse deserved all the praise I could heap on her.

Rye grass and clover grew together profusely and when the holding paddock was set aside for a month in November it grew pasture up to a foot in height. When mown the entwined foliage left strips like carpet.

Tractors were becoming more available and, while horses were still used, the end of the era of hard work for the draught Clydesdale was near. We had a power-driven mower operated from the tractor that had been purchased for planting the crops. Apart from the inconvenience of the frequent breaking of mowing blades, the mowing was completed successfully in one day.

I used a horse-drawn hay rake to collect the hay in rows ready to be collected for baling, and Bell performed both these tasks, obeying my commands but at her pace. The rake was designed to loose-roll the hay and send it into windrows, enabling easy collecting with the pickup prongs.

Hay rake

Bell knew only one pace and that was brisk, which meant that when using the hay rake one had to be quick with the pedal trip. We would rake the hay into windrows and leave it for some days to dry before baling.

We set up the baler in the middle of the paddock and brought the hay to it by a simple pronged fork collector sweep pulled by an enthusiastic Bell. It was a difficult task to keep her in check and an easy one to irritate the men feeding the baler, because while my attention was concentrated on the correct place, they needed to be on watch as I came in with each load.

The baling task took a team of men feeding, two tying, two removing and one on the collection rake. This last was usually my job as I knew Bell's moods better than anyone else and could anticipate any impending circumstance that might arise and most times nip it in the bud.

A board with grooves separated each bale and it would take skill to place it in the baler channel before the next action of the ram. The tying twine, fed automatically from a roll, would be threaded through top and bottom grooves in the slab. I can't remember how the baling twine was threaded through the top and bottom grooves and then, after cutting, tied by the man on the other side. But I can remember that the twine was around the length of the bale. If a tie was missed the bale flayed out at the end of the chute and had to be returned to the hay pile. It was the task of the person taking completed bales from the chute to the stacker to return the boards to the operator to be used again. Extra boards were used for backup allowing for hassle-free running off the baling operation.

Old baler, often driven by an old engine such as the one (right) restored by my brother, Bill

It was a dirty job, as the hay became dusty and each time the compressor ram completed its cycle, a cloud of dust would shower over everyone. By the end of the day we would all be covered in dust, and itchy. We blamed the rye grass that grew profusely among the clover. When cut, the mown hay would look like strips of green lying on the ground. The smell of new-mown hay is to everyone's liking except the hay fever sufferer.

The farmer had some grandiose dreams that he never fully realised. One was to go into hay baling in a big way and to this end he bought an expensive pick-up baler. The first one in the district, it was equipped with a double operation needle and self-threading of the wire. Two persons sat on a seat alongside each other, one cutting the wire and making a loop in it while the other threaded the wire end through the loop and twisted it to secure the bale sufficiently to allow for carrying without coming undone. Two ties to the bale and seven bales a minute meant no time to look up, and when the baler finished we would have no idea where we were in the paddock. If the stationary baler was described as a cloud of dust, the pickup baler dust is better described as a whirlwind, and if you weren't careful the cut wire played havoc with your fingers.

Later I believe that they improved to automatic wire tying and then to automatic string tying, but we didn't enjoy that luxury.

The oat crop we grew one year was ripening fast and a close watch was being kept to ensure the right time to harvest. Unlike wheat and barley that hold the grain heads for days and longer, the oats shed within hours and needed to be harvested on the day it ripened. Headers were now the way of harvesting the grain and a few people had them for contract harvesting. It was Christmas Day just after nine when I got the message that the crop was due for harvest at eleven.

I hastily changed into my work clothes and rode my *Malvern Star* bike the seventeen miles to the paddock. When the harvest began I spent hours bag-sewing the oats, barely keeping up to the bags that were filled each round or, in other places, when the header hopper was full. Bulk handling was in the future. Bags were sown with ears to make for easier handling and were stood ears-up for collection. Flat top trailers made for easy loading, with escalators for loading yet to come. Collecting and loading of bales became much easier, but in my time loading for transport and stacking was by manhandling.

LOADING THE BALES AND STACKING

We loaded the bales onto the trailer and then made a stack on a flat surface near the woolshed. As with the stacking of the sheaves of wheat and oat stacks, so too with the binding of the bales; skill was required by the stack-makers to ensure that the stack was held together.

As bales were passed from the trailer, each layer was laid differently and the higher the stack the harder the work for those on the trailer. When the stack was finished a ladder was used to bring the makers down from the ridge. Our stack was of seven layers on the base and five for the roof.

We ran pure bred Merino sheep and were heavily stocked. Feed ran low at the end of autumn and into early spring, and this was the time we fed bales to most of the sheep, especially the ewes due to drop their spring lambs.

Dray cart

Harnessing spirited Bell, who was always eager for a brisk trot in the dray cart, I would load up with bales and take them to the V-shaped feeders in the paddocks and top them up with fresh bales. If the hay from the previous top-up had run out, a flock of hungry sheep would come running, bleating and leaping at the back of my load behind me. If this was the case I would tease out a few bales and scatter them out behind me. Normally I would avoid this as much of the hay would be trodden into the ground and be wasted.

Circumstances saw me move to northern New South Wales and it was there I completed my apprenticeship by assisting in the harvesting of wheat on the river flats of the Severn River at Ashford and the irrigated paddocks below the Bonshaw Weir on the Dumaresq River in Queensland.

My early knowledge stood me in good stead when I took the opportunity to go from working for others to being a sharefarmer in Queensland and I cultivated and harvested crops for my dairy cows. In the 1950s before the time of bulk handling and before silos, cultivating was time-consuming, and tractors didn't have canopies to keep out the cold and dust.

I had the opportunity to keep up with the changes when on leave from my later job as a meat inspector in the Department of Primary Industries. After I retired I lent a friend a hand to harvest his lucerne with machinery capable of making large square bales or round ones and with a front-end loader on the tractor to transport them for shed storage.

My brother-in-law was a wheat farmer and, in my early retirement, I helped him with his wheat, which was loaded directly from the header to the bins on tip trucks for delivery to the storage silos at the railway line. Before the wheat was unloaded, samples were taken to determine quality and moisture content, and then the load was taken to the right silo and the grain unloaded onto the conveyer belts. The days of bagged wheat, I knew, were over.

Eighty years after my initiation into the agronomy field, my love of the smell of new-mown hay still stands. To satisfy that, I can rely on my self-drive and ride-on mowers when I mow the lawn at St John's Church, Oxley, and the spring clover is in full growth.

My trusty ride-on and motor mowers, St John.'s Church, Oxley

I still fancy myself as a skilled user of the scythe and sickle and I feel that I have earned a degree from the University of Hard Knocks.

Alan Smith

Offcuts 2

Peter Darmody

Brian Goeldner

BILL THIRKILL

CAMPING TOURS OF RUSSIA IN THE SIXTIES

Going on a camping tour in the sixties was so much fun for the under-30s in Europe, with lots of wonderful sights and in company with like-minded fun-loving people. There were so many good times, and for some new drinks to try out and songs to sing on the bus.

I am Bill, Bloody Bill to those who knew me. I was a tour manager/driver and all us drivers had nicknames. My main route was the north, taking in Scandinavia and Russia. This job entailed ensuring all had correct visas, organising the food and accommodation, teaching the other drivers about the cities and politics of each country we entered, handing the currency of each country to the driver the night before the border, reminding them which side of the road to drive on (Sweden was on the left, Norway the right — take care). I usually had four 16-seater buses.

The cities like Amsterdam, Hamburg and Copenhagen were really good fun places and set the mood for the trip, then on to Oslo and Stockholm as passengers got to know each other. Some, in fact, finished the trip with lifelong friends. As the 28-day trip progressed, they really enjoyed each other's company.

In some of my trips singing in the bus was the fun thing, starting off with the song *Tulips in Amsterdam* as we came into Holland, and *Wonderful Copenhagen* for Denmark. However, as the Seekers were a popular group in Australia and the other countries, their songs were sung a lot of times.

For the Australians and Kiwis, all new to all these amazing countries, it was endless enjoyment and fun. The Brits seemed to have a talent to find something to complain about, but all in good spirit and they could certainly sing well, lots of times too. Americans asked too many questions.

Our tours were summertime only, as camping in the winter was not possible. We saw incredible sites such as ski jumps, beautiful lakes and rivers and very historic buildings, but mostly enjoyed the night life of various cities.

The crossing of the Baltic Sea to Finland was a time to think about what was ahead, because after Helsinki in Finland we were to enter Russia. What would that be like?

After the joy of Helsinki, we had a good night driving along and overlooking the Gulf of Finland. Then we were on a not-so-good road to the Finnish border plus about a kilometre of no-man's-land to the Russian border. The border guards were very cranky-looking, chubby blokes in uniform, with hammer and sickle badges on their hats. They conducted a thorough check of each passenger and their visas, except for me! They knew me from before.

'Ah, Villiam,' they said, 'vot are you smuggling? Ve vil find it.'

So, the big search was on. They seemed to know that I was hiding illegal things, but didn't find them. Next, I had to change money at a little over two roubles for the pound. Everything was quite expensive, and we had to buy insurance as Western insurance did not cover us in Russia and was compulsory.

Hammer and sickle badge of Russian border guard

We moved on through a few kilometres of forest, sometimes seeing a bear or two. The first town in Russia was Viborg. All passengers went into shock as the contrast between the beautiful places we had been and now. There was such a difference — cobblestone roads in shocking condition, houses of logs and unpainted timber, no cars and just a few trucks.

The things that the group wanted to buy were Russian dolls and balalaikas, but most of all the vodka, which was quite cheap, but if you wanted orange to go with it, awfully expensive. We had to employ a guide full-time and he made sure we saw only the good things, although St Petersburg (formerly Leningrad) was quite good. It is built on a swamp so has many bridges.

We took three days to reach Moscow, where we spent a remarkably interesting five days. Then it was on to Minsk, Warsaw, Berlin and London.

We found that ballpoint pens were not available in Russia so when I was in London, I bought several boxes at about 18 shillings for a box of 144 to sell on the tour. I could sell them at one rouble each. I also found that the Bank of England needed to offload their roubles and they sold me some at 10 pence each if I bought 5000 at a time.

It was highly illegal to bring Russian money into that country, so we took a risk. All went well for a few trips and the pens sold very well. I also sold roubles to the passengers at the rate of twelve for 5 pounds.

Selling the pens was a priority as I needed the money to run the tour. So the first night in Leningrad I would take my people to the opera (a very boring thing), then set up my shop outside. A very long queue grew quickly, and I sold hundreds of pens.

However, the day came when I had a new American driver on #2 bus and he tried to cash a 100-rouble note I'd bought from the Bank of England. We were in trouble. We were both arrested. I had a big wad of notes which I stuffed behind a sign on the back of the bus, a 52-seat coach this time, as the police closed in.

The night was a very tough one of constant interrogation, with very loud yelling and me making up stories to tell via a very beautiful Russian girl who spoke perfect English. (She was the one who sold me insurance at the border). They eventually believed my story that I had changed money with a Finnish driver who left at the time I was arriving. I was fined the equivalent of 500 pounds and allowed to carry on with my tour, and they did not find my big wad of money.

There were a few problems with police as sometimes I did not understand the road signs. The day came when I was stopped by a big fat copper who took his book out and yelled loudly at me. My passengers became very quiet. I could hear some saying, 'Bill is getting booked.'

I asked the fat policeman, 'DO YOU SPEAK ENGLISH?'

He replied, 'Nyet' ('No.').

Then I said, 'You're an ugly looking bugger, aren't you?'

My people roared laughing. The copper quickly closed his book and took off.

Another problem was fuel. All cars and most trucks were on petrol so there were very few garages selling diesel fuel. So I had to top up at every opportunity as the garages with diesel were many hundreds of kilometres apart.

There was a time I got into trouble as my fuel was running out and we still had a hundred kilometres to go. A short time later I stopped at a shop and bought a four-litre drum of kerosene, made up a cardboard funnel and poured it in. All the local people were going crazy trying to warn me. They didn't know about diesel vehicles, and thought I had a petrol bus. I kept pouring. Then to the shock of the people I started the bus and drove off, with a lot of pinging from the engine, but it got me about fifty kilometres to the next garage.

Few cars were on the highways as people were very poor, so we drove quite quickly. As we entered Belarus, we were required to drive through a pit containing some type of disinfectant. We had to drive over a speed bump, quietly drive into the pit, then out again four metres away.

One day, while speeding along, I was lucky to see the disinfection pit ahead and went into the water nice and slowly, then stopped the other side to warn our following bus. I could see the yellow bus coming at speed and tried to stop him. However he never even slowed down, and hit the bump at 110 kph, lifting the bus well above the pit, but the roof rack even higher.

He landed well past the pit before stopping, but his roof rack kept going. The prongs broke off in the bitumen and gear went flying everywhere. Many of the purchased balalaikas were still in good condition, but much of our food was ruined. Our American driver was scolded by his passengers, and I then had to carry a much bigger load on my rack.

The tour continued to Minsk, Warsaw and Berlin. We left very early for the drive to London and arrived at about 11 am the following day. I would have a cleanup and a sleep, then leave the same day about 7 pm for the next tour.

As cold set in up north, I went on to drive the Middle East tours via Turkey, Syria, Lebanon, Jordan, Israel and other places, where I faced some big challenges.

All up I drove buses through about fifty countries. Later in life I did many African tours, but with a much older passenger group and different problems.

LUNCH WITH KING HUSSEIN

One day I was in North Africa enjoying a magnificent banquet lunch with King Hussein of Jordan and chatting to his wife Queen Noor. You may well wonder how this happened, so I'll tell you.

I had a small group of tourists on a camping tour of the Middle East. We were in the Hashemite Kingdom of Jordan. My vehicle was a twelve-seater transit bus. It had a roof rack where I kept our tents, stretchers and cooking gear, plus bags with their personal items. I had to load all this every day unless we were staying more than one night at any place.

One day we left early from Amman, the capital of Jordan, and followed the Desert Highway south towards Aqaba, but then turned west en route. We were heading to Petra, one of the world's most famous archaeological sites.

As we were approaching we saw a beautiful rainbow. We missed the accompanying storm but it was so nice to see such a sight in the red-coloured desert, which was very rocky. On arrival at Petra we found the storm had been quite fierce and the damage was quite visible.

I soon took my group to the gorge which is the entrance to the lost city. As we started walking we had to step over several donkeys drowned in the storm. The gorge is about one and a half metres wide with quite high red rock sides. No wonder the city was lost for hundreds of years.

My group really enjoyed seeing a most incredible sight, as the buildings are cut out of rock walls. It really is an amazing place, and many photos were taken.

After returning through the gorge we met up with some wonderful men of the Arab Legion. Their uniforms included bandoliers strung with bullets, and their horses were really beautiful.

Arab Legion of Jordan [1]

We viewed the stables and many interesting military pieces of equipment. Then I asked if my group could sleep in the stables. The soldiers agreed to this, which saved finding a place to put up our tents. So out came the stretchers and cooking gear and we settled in for the night with the Arab Legion.

It was a really interesting night as the men showed us their gear. They carried primus stoves so cooked their meal as we did, with our gas burners.

The following morning the town seemed to be excessively decorated with red carpets. We were told that the king was coming to open the new hospital so we must wait where we were for him to pass.

We did not wait long before the king with his entourage came, accompanied by the town's important people. He stopped when he saw our group (we were the only white people there). We

---

1 United States Library of Congress's Prints and Photographs division, www.loc.gov/pictures/item/2019712990

looked a scruffy lot. He asked who we were and started talking to me. We chatted for some time, and he told me of his American-born wife. Then he invited us all to join him for lunch.

King Hussein and Queen Noor of Jordan with President & Nancy Reagan, 1981[2]

We accepted with thanks, then told him of our lack of good clothes for such an auspicious occasion. He said, 'That's okay. Just do the best you can.'

And we did. In fact the women looked quite good after scrubbing up and in clean clothes.

We arrived at the venue at the given time of 12.30 pm, to be treated to the most magnificent banquet. We met the king's wife, Queen Noor, who was delighted we were there as it seemed she sometimes needed some English-speaking company. My passengers all had the best feed of the tour.

As for my chatting to his wife — well, I had a really great offer from one of my girls so left King Hussein with Noor. I married Fran soon after arriving in London two weeks later. The tour had gone for eleven weeks so we really knew each other well by then.

---

2 Wikimedia Commons, https://catalog.archives.gov/id/75856255

The wedding was at a registry office and we had a small reception at a friend's home with some of the travelling group. The cost at the registry office was twelve shillings. I think I had good value as we are still happily married 55 years later.

A sad footnote is that about two months after meeting our friends of the Arab Legion, they were all dead. They could not match the modern enemy forces that invaded Jordan at this time.

THE LURE OF THE DEEP

When I was about 40, my son Peter and I were really enjoying our times around Moreton Bay in our boat and the company of many other boating friends.

However, there was another aspect of the water which was still a mystery to us: what is under us?

So, Peter and I decided to take up scuba diving. We enrolled in a course, passed all the theory and shallow dives in Chandler swimming pool and the Tweed River, then did our first open water dives at Julian Rocks, Byron Bay. These were 30-metre dives, and the water visibility was not good, and we did get a bit worried going down the anchor rope when a large shark came near us. However, the bottom was really interesting as there was a big cave full of fish and a giant groper, which came out as I entered.

We did five dives there, and were presented with our open water diver qualification card. After that we bought our own gear and started to do dives at many places.

Mooloolaba became our favourite local dive as there are the remains of a volcano about ten kilometres south-east, and the dive can be either inside or outside the crater. Inside is incredible. On returning to the surface one time we came across a school of

Sketches and Stories from the Shed

tuna about six metres down, so we joined them for quite some time until we saw two tiger sharks following. We dropped back to the bottom until they were gone.

We also dived Lady Musgrave Island for a week, really beautiful dives and amazing fish life. However I was now eager to see more, and shipwrecks were now my ambition. The Solomon Islands had plenty.

A good friend called Tony and I set about getting to see these. First a flight to Guadalcanal where we were able to dive the wreck of a B-17 bomber in quite good condition, except the tail section was broken and hanging down. We were able to enter there and swim through to the cockpit. Wonderful. All the crew had survived but the Japanese had cut their heads off.

There were other wrecks of ships and many places of interest from the Second World War, all of which were really worth seeing.

A flight in a Twin Otter came next, to an island called Ghizo (and the town of Gizo) in the Solomon Islands, near Bougainville, where many great dives were to be enjoyed. The shock came as soon as we entered the terminal as the smell of the local people waiting to board was overpowering, but we had a really beautiful flight.

The hotel was run by a very wise man called Charlie, a quite tall guy, very black, who always had lots of people wanting to chat with him and share his wisdom, a really likeable guy. He had a beautiful white girlfriend, a Kiwi doctor.

The first dive was a cargo ship laying upright on the bottom about 30 metres down which had small Japanese tanks on board. It had a torpedo hole which I could get through and make my way to the decks above, past the galley, which was still set with plates and cups and Saki bottles. A great dive.

There were war planes and other ships but then we went to the island where President Kennedy was during the war. Just off shore in about twenty feet of water was a Hellcat fighter from a carrier, with bullet holes that may have killed the pilot.

He must have crash-landed as the plane was in quite good condition. The dashboard had all the instruments, and the guns were loaded. I sat in the seat and felt the moment of the crash.

All the transport for us divers were long canoes with 20-horsepower outboards. They went through amazingly rough water no problem, even though some of these craft had very big people on board and lots of them too.

Some months later we took a flight to Port Moresby in PNG and then to Madang, where we stayed at a beautiful hotel overlooking the harbour. There were more wrecks to be explored, one being a B-25 bomber about twenty-five metres down on a crazy angle on a reef. It had torpedoes and many bombs aboard, the guns were loaded, and the port engine was missing. I sat in the pilot seat but could hardly see over the dash. (Pilots sit on their parachutes when in action.)

We met many locals and went out to their villages and watched them climb the palms for betel nuts. There was also a Japanese bomber which they had left behind, and some other ordnance.

It was a very interesting and worthwhile experience, and we knew a bit more about 'what is under us'.

AFRICA AND ORANGES

When I retired from my trade as a plumber in 2002, the word got out, and I had various offers to help use my free time. I did not need these. However, I was contacted by an old friend, Dick, who was in the travel industry and knew my background as a tour manager. He informed me he needed a driver for Africa, an offer I firmly refused.

However, a few months later, during a night out with our wives and many beers, he asked me again in a very pleading manner. This time I couldn't refuse him, and I began driving in Africa in 2009.

In September 2013 I was with a tour that began in Cape Town, South Africa. My first task was to show the city and surrounding towns, Stellenbosch, Cape of Good Hope and so on. However, there was a minor problem at some traffic lights: when I stopped the bus at a red light, we would be bombarded with vendors selling all sorts of things.

I had to admire the patience of other motorists — when a deal was being done with a driver up front and the lights turned green, there were no horns used. The other cars just waited until the deal was done, money and goods handed over, and then all moved on. So nice.

I thought some things might be handy for making deals during the tour, so at one set of lights I bought several bags of oranges. I could give some to my passengers and keep some for any other purpose that might arise.

We left Cape Town and headed north, crossed into Namibia, and did the tour sites, including the Fish River Canyon, which is almost 550 metres deep in places and quite amazing. The bus blew a couple of tyres in the Kalahari desert. We kept heading north, passing many villages with different tribes of people, all with different languages.

Then on to Windhoek, the capital. As Namibia had been a German colony, many spoke German. I took everyone to a beer house, where they tried the local drop, which was really very much like a German beer. They had a great night.

We kept heading north, calling into a great park and seeing many animals and birds, then north again to a city where the local tribe was the Herero. The women dressed like the missionaries of the 19th century, with long flowing frocks.

As it happened there was a buggy pulled by four donkeys taking a well-dressed family to town using a track at the side of the main road. They were moving quite quickly and my passengers were trying to get a photo. Well, the ORANGES!

Family buggy pulled by four donkeys

I pulled out a bag of oranges, moved to a spot ahead of the family, pulled up and offered them the fruit. They stopped and gratefully accepted the oranges, and my passengers and I got really nice photos. When we carried on into town, it was so clean and orderly and for us a pleasure to be there, wandering around.

We moved on and the next tribe we met up with, the Kavango, were quite the opposite to the Herero people because clothes were missing on many parts we are used to covering. The town was chaotic, too dangerous for me to let my passengers roam around.

Heading north again through more parks, my passengers seemed to be fascinated by the families of meercats — all busy and the little ones enjoying playing with each other. Moving on we came across a school, so I stopped to talk to some women who were in the shade of a tree with a pot of something cooking on a fire. This was tuck shop for the kids.

Cooking food for the schoolchildren's lunch

So out came the oranges which were very gratefully accepted. When I asked if we could meet the children, a lady was very obliging and took us into the class room. After the initial shock that the children had on seeing us, they decided to sing to us. Their singing was magnificent — the lead singer would start, then all would follow, then more from the lead and all joined in.

We stopped at some walled settlements, all with rondavel huts (small cylindrical houses with a conical thatched roof), and shared more oranges with lovely people.

A rondavel hut, and another sharing of oranges

The next day we stopped at a guest house on the Okavango River. Over the river was the country of Angola. This area was a no-go place and it was illegal to cross the river. However, my people wanted to do something a bit daring.

A young guy was holding a boat to tie it up, and when I showed him the oranges he agreed to take us across. About eight of us boarded and, sitting on what looked like a kitchen chair, the young guy held the tiller and took us across. One of the women made up a sign saying 'Illegal boat people', and when we jumped off the boat on the other shore they took photos holding the sign. Then it was quickly on to the boat and back across the river.

I had run out of oranges so no more bribes could be done, and there were still a couple of weeks to go — to Botswana, Zimbabwe (Victoria Falls), more animals, on to Sun City Resort in South Africa, then it was Johannesburg and goodbye to everyone.

The next year Dick had a problem with diabetes and lost his legs as a result. So the company was sold, to a buyer from Zimbabwe. The new people did not need an Australian tour manager, but I found that there were still other things in life for me.

Sketches and Stories from the Shed

David – Anthony Durrington

Contributors

TREVOR ARMSTRONG was born in Ipswich in 1948, shortly after his twin sister, Heather. With five other siblings, he grew up on the family's 1,000-acre dairy farm, which stretched from the Seven Mile, east of Rosewood, across the Bremer River to Ebenezer. Trevor progressed from early milk deliverer to sprinter and long distance runner, and played representative soccer and rugby league. After graduation, he worked for the Queensland Department of Lands/Natural Resources, Mines and Energy, and specialised for over 30 years as the Land Protection Division's *Alan Fletcher Research Station* Agronomist. Since retiring in 2006, Trevor has concentrated on coordinating opportunities for improving sustainable ecological practices to mitigate climate change.

WILLIAM BARKER, the third eldest of nine brothers and one sister, grew up in Brisbane. He was conscripted for compulsory National Service in 1966, eventually serving from May 1968 for two years in the Royal Australian Army Service Corps. William was posted to Nui Dat, Vietnam, from May 1969 to May 1970. After National Service, he took up primary school teaching and principalship. He married Mary in 1973 and they have a daughter and three sons, thirteen grandchildren and two great-grandsons. On retirement, he commenced wood-turning and took up traditional rocking-horse carving. His stories are for his children and grandchildren.

JOHN BROWN was raised in the Great Depression and left school at age fourteen. He has an agricultural background, working sheep and cattle properties in Victoria and New South Wales as well as dairy farming in Queensland. He has three children, seven grandchildren and ten great-grandchildren. He reached senior level by correspondence and became a Stock and Meat Inspector. John retired as Senior Inspector in charge of slaughterhouses, pet food and butchers' shops in 1987, and continued to play an active role in the church and community. Encouraged by the support of then-Councillor Milton Dick, he founded the Oxley Community Men's Shed in 2011.

PETER DARMODY grew up on a sheep farm in the Monaro district of southern New South Wales. He studied in Sydney to become a high school teacher, but in 1967 he was called up for National Service and was posted to Papua New Guinea as an army education instructor. After National Service he worked initially as a teacher and then as an economist, mainly in Canberra. He has been drawing and painting for over 20 years and enjoys sketching on holidays and around Brisbane. Examples of Peter's work can be found on Instagram (@petedarmody_art).

Despite the early disappointment of not winning a competition for his shark painting when he was four years old, **ANTHONY DURRINGTON** continued his artistic pursuits. A potter since 1988, he has also tried his hand at drawing, photography, graphic design and sculpture, even briefly dipping his toe into the world of glass-blowing and blacksmithing. The earth has turned full circle and after an almost 50-year hiatus he has returned to painting. He is looking forward to seeing where this leads him.

DARRYL DYMOCK is Convenor of the Writers Group at Oxley Men's Shed. He's also a mentor with the Queensland Writers Centre and an Adjunct Senior Research Fellow at Griffith University. Darryl has had eleven different occupations to date, including taxi driver, Army education instructor and university lecturer. He lived and worked in three Australian states and PNG, and finally ended up back in Brisbane, his hometown, with his wife and his laptop. They have four children and seven grandchildren. Darryl is a published author and blogs occasionally at https://drdymockwriter.com.

BRIAN GOELDNER was born in Brisbane in 1949, the eldest of four children. He is married with two daughters and four grandchildren. For 46 years he worked as a baker/pastrycook, owning the *Market Cake Shop* in Rocklea for 10 years, then *Dominiques* in Ipswich City Square. After retiring in 2012, Brian and his wife travelled extensively overseas. Since joining Oxley Men's Shed, he has very much enjoyed the camaraderie there, and through the drawing group has found a new outlet for his creativity.

JIM PASCOE has spent the over sixty years in the Corinda and Oxley area. His entire career was spent in the electrical distribution network, starting his apprenticeship with the Brisbane City Council, Electricity Department, which became SEQEB, then Energex. He had a varied career in many departments before retiring as Technical Support Officer at the Call Centre. He was a member of the Royal Australian Navy Reserve until he married. He met his wife Janice in Warwick, where he spent the majority of his weekends. They have four children and thirteen grandchildren. He has been a member of the Oxley Men's Shed since its inception.

GEORGE PUGH lives with his wife Lorraine in Inala, Brisbane. They have two children, six grandchildren and one great-grandchild. George retired in 2000 after 36 years in the Queensland Police Service. He was a third-generation police officer, having followed in the footsteps of his father and his grandfather. During his police service, George was awarded the Queen's Commendation for Brave Conduct for his actions during the recapture of an escaped prisoner. After retirement George has been enjoying caravanning trips with his wife and attending the Oxley Men's Shed. He says that joining the Shed was the best decision he ever made.

DAVE SHEARER's life started as a country boy in 1945 in South Australia, with five older siblings. At age 16 he joined the Army as an apprentice fitter and turner, then moved on to Army Aviation, training in aircraft maintenance in Queensland, and 15 months operational service in Vietnam. Dave married in 1970, and he and his wife have four children and six grandchildren. Following his discharge in 1971, he worked in Adelaide for Australia Post, then in South Australia and Queensland with the Federal Government Lighthouse Service as a mechanic. When the Service was privatised, he obtained a gas fitting licence and worked in this area until his retirement.

ALAN SMITH was born in 1945. His parents had a fruit and vegetable farm at Upper Brookfield, then a remote outer area of Brisbane. He went to the local school until grade 8, then to Indooroopilly State High. At the end of Grade 10 (then called Junior), he started an apprenticeship as a Motor Mechanic. After injuring his back while working on a marine diesel engine, he was able to transfer to a second apprenticeship as an instrument technician. That job folded after eight years, but he was fortunate to get a position with the RACQ, where he worked for 30 years before retiring in 2008.

BILL THIRKILL grew up in Brisbane and did an apprenticeship to become a plumber. He moved to France to do skydiving in the world championships, then became a tour manager, where he met his wife Fran. They were engaged in Israel and married in England, then moved to New Zealand, and finally to Australia. They have three children. On his return to Australia, Bill took up plumbing again, but retired at age 60 when his son Peter took over the plumbing business. Eventually Bill went back to tour driving, this time in Africa. He has driven coach tours through 54 countries.

JAMES VERNON had a variety of interests and occupations before his retirement. He trained to be a French horn player; had his own photographic studio; studied to be a high school teacher, and finally became a teacher of English to speakers of other languages and examiner for the International English Language Testing System. These occupations were interspersed with two periods of boredom in the public service. Now he is retired and spends his days reading, writing and pursuing his interest in photography. Life is good.

Feet up – Anthony Durrington

www.ingramcontent.com/pod-product-compliance
Lightning Source LLC
Chambersburg PA
CBHW041317110526
44591CB00021B/2819